# SPLASH!

## A Leader's Guide to Effective Public Speaking

OBSTACLES PRESS

First Edition, January 2014
10 9 8 7 6 5 4 3 2 1

Published by:

Obstaclés Press
4072 Market Place Dr.
Flint, MI 48507

OBSTACLÉS
PRESS

life-leadership-home.com

ISBN 978-0-9913474-1-4

*Cover design and layout by Norm Williams, nwa-inc.com*

Printed in the United States of America

# SPLASH!

## A Leader's Guide to
## Effective Public Speaking

**LIFE Leadership Essentials Series**

**Foreword by Chris Brady**

# CONTENTS

# FOREWORD

## by Chris Brady

I sat in my little metal folding chair absolutely petri-
fied. My hands were sweaty, my posture slumped,
and I couldn't hear a word the presenter was saying.
All my faculties were consumed with the fear of my im-
pending doom.

What was so downright terrifying?

I was about to give my first official public presentation!

I was eighteen years old and an engineering co-op
student at General Motors. More for our benefit than
anything else, at the end of each semester, we co-op
students were required to give a review of our work
assignments and accomplishments that term.

They were despicable affairs, to be sure, with a dim
little old-fashioned bulb-type overhead projector and
amateur flimsies comprised of lots of really unimportant
information. One by one, each victim would get up and
grind through a horrid three minutes.

Soon it would be my turn.

My memory blanks at this point. Perhaps it's some sort
of protection mechanism, the kind of thing that eliminates
our past tragedies from memory or at least preserves
our self-image by refusing to remind us of times when
we made complete fools of ourselves! At any rate, I can't

recall one detail about that presentation except for how scared I was beforehand.

This condition didn't go away anytime soon, either. Year after year, we went through the same drill, and I was just as scared each time.

* * *

Fast forward to today, where I basically make my living speaking in front of audiences around the world. I give approximately fifty public talks a year to audiences of all sizes and have been doing so (and often more) for almost twenty years. Now, I don't even break a sweat. I am not only *not* scared by speaking in public; I actually relish each moment!

What happened?

If you're like me at all, you probably can relate to the fear and trepidation I describe above. For some reason, most of us feel that way when we're asked (or forced) to get up in front of a group and deliver any kind of message.

For me, the fear gradually dried up as I found myself in business for myself and confronted by the necessity of delivering information to other people through the spoken word. The proverbial "time on the water" did a lot to calm my nerves and make me feel comfortable speaking in front of a crowd.

But overcoming the fear of public speaking is only one part of the equation. The second, much bigger consideration is to overcome the tendency that afflicts almost all public speakers at some point in their development— namely, that of being boring and ineffective. Sadly, it seems as if the vast majority of public presentations are somewhere between merely adequate and downright sleep-inducing. There are reasons for this.

In the pages to follow, you will become acquainted with specific steps you can take to put together and deliver engaging, entertaining, informative, and inspiring public talks. You will be encouraged to practice your ability to speak in public (by doing it *often*—the only sure way to finally get rid of those nerves) and equipped with the principles and specifics of how to make your talks truly effective.

I am convinced that public speaking is something *anyone* can master. As with many other things in life, it doesn't really matter where you start but only that you *do* actually start! And once you've thus begun, the goal is to improve as quickly as you can. Put the thoughts and concepts in this book to work for you, and take your public speaking to a whole new level.

Finally, imagine a speaker getting ready for a major speech to a large audience in a full arena.

*He feels no nerves, no worries. Instead, he is excited to share his message. As the time for his speech arrives, he gets ready to go onstage.*

*He listens to the current speaker, taking notes and thinking about how to apply what she's saying to his own situation. When they call for the break, he smiles and stands up. A friend walks past and asks, "Are you ready?"*

*"Ready for what?" he asks curiously.*

*"For your speech?"*

*"Oh." He is genuinely surprised.*

*"What are you going to speak about?" the friend asks while the technician attaches the microphone to the speaker's belt and tie.*

*"I've got a new concept I want to share," he says. Then he asks about his friend's work and family. He hasn't seen him for a while.*

*When the master of ceremonies reopens the convention, he pulls out his note cards and glances at his outline. He's been through it so many times in his mind that he doesn't get past the first line. He immediately starts thinking of better ways to share it.*

*He stops himself, puts the note cards into his briefcase, and then leaves it on the table. He walks to the side of the stage, ready to head up the stairs to speak. He can see part of the audience from his vantage point, and he can already feel their energy, which only adds to his own excitement to share this vital message with them. "I love this!" he says to himself. "I can't imagine being anywhere I'd like better."*

*"This is so much fun. I'm ready to speak...."*

And you will be too. This is the goal for great speakers, along with delivering a transformational speech that really makes a difference to everyone in the audience. This is what we call SPLASH speaking. It's something we can all work toward as speakers, and it's what this book is all about.

Your audience awaits!

# INTRODUCTION

Beginning public speakers usually think there are three main types of speakers: good, bad, and somewhere in between. Advanced speakers—those who really know how to read every crowd, speak to each person's heart and mind in a way that moves them deeply, and leave the listeners forever changed—see speaking differently.

For top leaders, public speaking is about SPLASH!

In truth, splashes are amazing. They cause immediate waves, followed by a lot of ripples. And in the process, many people get wet or even muddy. If you've ever visited Sea World and watched the giant splashes from the whales arch far into the sky and then drench a stadium full of people, you know what a successful speech is all about.

In fact, if you watch a Sea World crowd, even the people far up in the top bleachers, who don't get a drop of water on them, react to each huge splash by jerking backward, covering their faces, and acting in other ways as if the wave were coming right at them.

Every drop from a big splash causes a series of ripples. People go home and share what they learned and, even more important, what they *felt*. SPLASH speaking is an essential part of what Chris Brady and Orrin Woodward call Level 5 Leadership: developing leaders who develop leaders.

Indeed, the memories created by effective SPLASH speaking endure for a lifetime.

Just think of the best speech you ever heard. Picture the event in your mind. Did you hear it in a stadium, at church, in the car, or somewhere else?

What made it so great? Was it the ambiance? The lighting and cheering? The message? An electric energy in the room? The force of nature that seemed to emanate from the speaker? The notes you took and how they changed you later? A specific quote or phrase that seemed to switch on a light bulb in your mind? Or something else?

Whatever your answer, one thing is certain. Great speeches, SPLASH speeches, leave you different than you were before you heard them. You feel something, and the feeling has a lasting impact on you and your life. The ripples of what you felt and learned during the speech continue in your life long after the big waves have come and gone.

Beginning speakers often try to "break the ice" by using jokes, visual aids, gimmicks, or other techniques to pique the interest of the audience. Top leaders know that there is a better way, that in fact, gimmicks are really just gimmicks and that the same joke or visual aid will be mediocre when used by a struggling speaker but burn a lasting memory when employed by a great speaker.

It's not the techniques, it's not just the preparation, and it's not even the message that matters most. It's the SPLASH that causes real change, that leaves listeners different, that ignites those in the crowd and sways their future.

So what exactly is SPLASH? In addition to symbolizing how to become a speaker who touches every person in the audience and leaves a lasting memory, SPLASH is an acronym for the following guidelines of truly effective speakers:

**S**ay something that matters.
**P**repare the speaker, not just the speech.
**L**eave it all backstage.
**A**udience is everything.
**S**implicity is power.
**H**appen!

Note that SPLASH speakers aren't born; they're made. It takes effort, practice, and repetition to become a great speaker. Sitting in an audience listening to a world-class speech, it is easy to get the false idea that the speaker is just plain gifted. Certainly, there are people with various gifts that help their public speaking, but nobody ever became an excellent speaker without hard work.

For example, attend a professional football game or a nationally recognized orchestra performance, and you'll be amazed at how some of the athletes and musicians make their work seem so simple. But what they do is actually far from easy. If you knew the long years of practice, workouts, lessons, failures, struggles, sweat, and effort that brought them to this moment, you'd be amazed.

Any true success is built on a genuine foundation of intense and consistent work.

The same is true of great speakers. That said, understanding SPLASH will help you fast-forward past years, even decades, of trial and error.

Mentoring is incredibly powerful for this very reason: An experienced mentor can help you jump ahead by applying his wealth of experience and skipping many hurdles along the way. This book is such a mentor for anyone who wants to become a truly good public speaker.

If you begin applying the principles of SPLASH speaking right now, today, your public speaking will start improving by leaps rather than baby steps.

There is an old saying that "practice makes perfect." This is actually only partially true. The reality is that the *right kind* of practice makes perfect. In other words, practicing skills incorrectly tends to *lessen* them and reduce your effectiveness.

Those who read this book and learn and apply the principles of SPLASH speaking can start practicing the right way, and this will drastically accelerate their learning curve. Moreover, if you have ever stressed about public speaking or felt nervous before a speech, SPLASH speaking will help you conquer your fear and forget about yourself.

Indeed, this is a hallmark of great speakers: They tend to forget about themselves and immerse their delivery in the needs of their audience. SPLASH speaking will teach you how to do this simply, immediately, and effectively.

There is much to learn, but becoming a better public speaker will help you in countless ways. So get ready to get wet—because a SPLASH is coming!

# Say Something That Matters

*Happiness is when what you think,*
*what you say, and what you do are in harmony.*
—Mahatma Gandhi

# 1

## *The best way to conquer stage fright is to know what you're talking about.*
—MICHAEL H. MESCON

Jerry Seinfeld famously said, "According to most studies, people's number one fear is public speaking. Death is number two. Does that sound right? This means to the average person, if you go to a funeral, you're better off in the casket than doing the eulogy."

This is a funny statement, but it's one many of us can relate to. When put in these terms, it seems highly unlikely that some people would rather die than give a speech, but research confirms that this is an accurate reference to real studies done in the United States.

While most people have never really been presented with the option to choose between death and public speaking, it is true that many of us feel a constant and real dread of standing in front of people to speak—while at the same time, we don't constantly worry about our own looming demise.

Interestingly enough, the list of people who fear public speaking is not limited to those who manage to avoid it. Even many of the best speakers admit to being terrified every time they walk out onstage. Yet they somehow manage to do it anyway. Why is that?

## Great Orator

In almost every story of a great hero, from modern movies to historical accounts and everything in between, public speaking has been an instrumental tool for winning battles of every kind—whether physical, emotional, or philosophical. Take great speeches out of the *Iliad*, the *Odyssey*, or the writings of Shakespeare, and the stories will be much less interesting and powerful.

The same is true of history, from speeches by Martin Luther to the excellent speeches of the American Civil War or those of Winston Churchill. Getting on your feet and making a beautiful or persuasive speech has always been one of the most powerful ways to call others to arms, both literally and figuratively. This is true for a number of reasons.

The first and most obvious reason is that if people have never heard or thought of your point, they're much less likely to agree with you than if they have. So to get them on *your* side, you have to show them the sides in the first place.

Second, when you're the one who stands and explains the sides of any battle, you are the one who defines the sides, which is both a huge advantage and a great responsibility. You have to give your audience some sense of the good and evil of the situation. And since you're the one doing it, you're likely to get more people to join *your* army than the opposing one.

The third reason is tied very closely to the fear of speaking that many of us experience. Since such a large number of us are afraid to stand up ourselves, we tend to give an extra level of respect, along with a listening ear, to those who are willing to brush past that fear and vocally stand up for what they believe.

Of course, not everyone who tries this is a skillful speaker but, as we said, the great orator is an archetype or icon that appears in almost every story of heroism and victory. While not every hero is a public speaker, impressive public speaking almost always influences the outcome of any great story.

Speaking is a tool that is capable of swaying hundreds and even thousands or millions of people to a cause of great importance. Likewise, it can be used to push these same thousands into insignificance, mediocrity, and apathy. Even worse, in some instances, it may be responsible for bringing death and destruction.

Speakers have enormous power to define the beliefs of their audiences for good or for bad because they are able to influence many at once and in such a deep way that is simultaneously emotional and intellectual. When delivered effectively, a speech can leave thousands of listeners firmly believing whatever ideas the speaker shares.

> *When delivered effectively, a speech can leave thousands of listeners firmly believing whatever ideas the speaker shares.*

## Speakers Are Warriors

That said, speakers must see themselves as what they are: warriors. This is the starting point of SPLASH speaking, of becoming a good public speaker. A person who gets up and speaks to thousands, hundreds, or even just a few people at a time must recognize that his or her role is not frivolous or light.

In reality, those who think this is a world of pink fluffy clouds, lollipop rain, and prancing unicorns should probably not be speaking. People with this kind of view are not likely to understand the weight of responsibility and power that falls on the shoulders of the warrior-speaker. Great public speakers are engaged in a battle of ideals—in topics from poverty or slavery to mediocrity or laziness.

> *Great public speakers are engaged in a battle of ideals— in topics from poverty or slavery to mediocrity or laziness.*

Public speaking is for people who recognize the war between excellence and mediocrity, freedom and force, good and evil. Public speaking is for those who have seen the sides, know the stakes, and have chosen a side.

In short, public speaking is for people who stand for something that truly matters. It is for those who have something to lose if their side fails and everything to gain when it wins. It is also for those who are just starting to realize that their life purpose can be remarkable, even if this level of intensity is new to them.

## But What about Seinfeld?

With this warrior-speaker thought in mind, let's lighten the mood a bit by looking back at the Seinfeld quote that opened this chapter. We've already discussed its merits and its truthfulness, but there's one more point to be considered: someone *does* have to give the eulogy.

And someone always does, even though that person is often scared silly. Yet many times, those who give eulogies speak very well, despite the circumstances. This occurs quite frequently because in such a situation, most speakers

> *Someone* **does** *have to give the eulogy.*

naturally stand for something. They truly care about what they're speaking about. That's why a eulogy is generally done by someone who was close to the deceased.

Such people aren't onstage because they happened to be the only one in the audience who had absolutely no fear of public speaking. They are there because they care so much about what they have to say that they're going to say it *even though* they're scared.

In this way, the best cure for stage fright is not only *knowing* what you're talking about but truly *caring* about it.

When it comes right down to it, if you don't care about your topic, you're not the one who should speak about it. Your delivery will probably be both painful and ineffective, even if you are generally an excellent public speaker in other settings.

Almost everyone suffers from stage fright, and for some, it is their worst fear. The first step to effective SPLASH speaking is to find something you care enough about to fight for it and defeat stage fright on a consistent basis.

This is true in many settings in our lives, especially in business and career, not just in public speaking. Those who care enough take action. Warriors are often afraid, but when the battle truly matters, they go forward boldly despite any fears.

Once you've embraced this concept, you're going to see instant improvements in your ability and motivation to speak. Until then, any speech you give will typically be lacking in conviction and power.

How, then, can you find a cause? The war for good is being fought on too many fronts to count. Which battle is yours? The answer is quite simple. When you know what really matters to you, you'll be ready to start becoming a SPLASH speaker.

> *When you know what really matters to you, you'll be ready to start becoming a SPLASH speaker.*

For example, do you care about families? About morality? About freedom or decency or children? Do you care about prosperity? Do you care about having more time to spend with your family or about fighting less over finances with your spouse? Do you care about your business message or the product you're selling? Do you care about that new initiative or project at work?

Different people care about different ideas, causes, and values. When you know what you care about, you take a huge leap toward becoming an excellent public speaker. We'll spend more time on this in the chapters ahead, but for now, simply ask yourself what you really, deeply care about in life.

When you apply this in both your personal and your professional life, you'll be on your way toward becoming a SPLASH speaker.

# 2

## *Let thy speech be better than silence, or be silent.*

—DIONYSIUS OF HALICARNASSUS

As you're picking a battle or purpose, it is essential that you don't just choose one you *do* care about but also one that you *should* care about. There are very few "battles" out there that are truly worthless, so this shouldn't be too hard. But be sure you're not picking something that doesn't have a deep and important meaning to you.

If the battle doesn't matter much, it really shouldn't matter to you, so move on. Pick on someone your own size. Put your weight and work where it will make a real difference in the world.

This really is a simple idea, yet we often tend to pour our lives and energy into trivial matters that really don't

> *Don't waste your efforts in the wrong place because the right place does exist.*

amount to much in the long run. This is tragic because so many other worthy causes (both big and small) are desperate for our support and help.

We've all heard the saying "Pick your battles," and leaders absolutely must do this. Otherwise, they are in danger of losing the battles that matter. The point is this: Don't waste your efforts in the wrong place because the right place does exist. If the war is important, then your contribution is too. Don't squander it.

## The General and Special Theory of Wasted Words

Obviously, this applies to the big picture and what causes you choose to dedicate your life to, but it is also significant on a more specific, case-by-case basis.

Once you've ruled out the unimportant causes and selected the one(s) you were born to stand behind, it's vital that you keep these in the forefront of your mind every time you make a decision.

Certain speaking engagements simply won't get you closer to achieving your success and accomplishing your goals. Those are the ones you should decline. Period.

Now sometimes you'll be required to give presentations or mini-speeches at work for some reason or other that might not seem to get you closer to your highest aims and goals. We aren't suggesting that you unnecessarily burn bridges or get yourself fired. But to be a truly great SPLASH speaker, you should never give a speech without understanding its role in your life vision and dreams.

If you're knowingly betraying your cause to fulfill someone else's assignment, you have a real problem. But sometimes, while certain venues or audiences might not seem to fit with your purpose, they are necessary steps along your journey, though the connections to the big picture may not be direct or obvious.

In any case, it is critical that you don't betray yourself, but rather find a way to turn these required projects into the building blocks of your success. Use them to make yourself a better speaker and thinker and to strengthen your most vital relationships.

As you do, you'll be framing these experiences in a way that puts *you* in charge and *them* in their proper place in your bigger picture and purpose.

## Pick *Deep*

Obviously, if what you're saying isn't important, you shouldn't be saying it. But it goes deeper. If having said something to a certain crowd or in a particular situation *won't* matter in the long run, then it's the same as if your message itself had no consequence.

This is called living with intention—utilizing the power of focus, beginning with the end in mind, and applying strategic effort or just plain smart work. Whatever you call it, it's the method used by effective leaders.

But let's get to how this applies in practical ways. If you know before a speech that nothing will be different when you sit down after talking, you should probably find a different audience or venue, or perhaps prepare yourself more. In any event, the idea is that you only say what matters and in ways that will matter.

If one of those two requirements isn't met, don't say it. The implementation of this one principle is what separates many great speeches from more mediocre ones. In other words, SPLASH speakers worry less about techniques or delivery than about the conse-quences of their message.

> *SPLASH speakers worry less about techniques or delivery than about the consequences of their message.*

We'll spend time in this book on techniques and delivery, to be sure, but the starting point is deeply caring about your message!

## Nonaction vs. Right Action

This doesn't mean that you should be consistently saying nothing. You may have the pessimistic idea that no matter what you say or do, your cause will ultimately fail; sadly, many people do. But if that's where you're at, you have a real problem, and it isn't just the ultimate failure of everything you care about.

First of all, if your cause truly matters, there is some-body who needs to hear about it, somebody who's ready to listen. Your job is to find the person(s) and be prepared to really influence them in the right ways.

If nobody needs your speech or your message, it's time to find a new one. Of course, when this seems to be the case, you need to be certain that you aren't just giving in to pressure from critics or caving in at the first sign of difficulty. Or the second. Or the eighty-seventh.

Be ready to endure some hardship for a cause that matters, and be willing to work long and hard to find success. That's usually part of the program for those who change their personal lives or the world for the better, and it is completely worth it.

## The Golden Mean

In summary, the way to really succeed as a speaker is to begin by getting your mind in the right place. Stephen Covey called this "beginning with the end in mind." This includes saying no to opportunities that won't get you closer to your ultimate success so you can spend your time and energy on the things that will.

Remember why you're doing what you're doing, and keep doing it. Once you are consistently doing the right things, you'll be well on the way to becoming a truly effective SPLASH speaker, and you'll be changing yourself and the world in small ways all along the way.

It all starts by clarifying the ideas, values, and causes you care about. Why are you giving a speech? Why do you want to be a better public speaker? If your reason for these things is that you want to promote something that really matters to you, you are well on your way.

# 3

## *Speech is power: speech is to persuade, to convert, to compel.*

—Ralph Waldo Emerson

We've already spent some time discussing the power and responsibility of public speaking. By now, you should understand that those who stand and speak in front of crowds should do so because they have something worthwhile to say, knowing that they might actually help others and even convince people to agree with them on important ideas.

That said, good speakers should plan their message accordingly and be ready to deal with the consequences.

As you set out to improve yourself and/or change the world, and specifically to change people's minds and hearts, it's essential to pay attention to who is influencing your own thoughts, feelings, and actions.

What speeches, books, TV shows, movies, people, blogs, newspapers, journals, or other media and personal sources are you allowing to shape and impact your message to the world? You're kidding yourself if you think you can experience them and somehow keep them from influencing you.

## The Media War

It's pretty likely that you hear, see, and internalize a lot of information that isn't worthy of a mighty warrior for families, prosperity, truth, liberty, success, or whatever it is you stand for. What are you doing to fight back?

What you put in is usually what you get out, as top leader Chris Brady puts it. We all understand this concept. It's the idea of, "Show me where you fish, and I'll show you what you'll catch." When you're preparing your message

> *"Show me where you fish, and I'll show you what you'll catch."*

and deciding what to stand for, you have a limited supply of things to work with—limited to the information, ideas, principles, thoughts, and feelings that are familiar and available to you.

If you don't know it, you probably won't ever say it in a speech. That said, one of the responsibilities of public speakers is to be careful what input they allow to persuade, convince, and compel them. You've got to be constantly fighting any negative information you encounter with truly excellent stuff that will keep you in the right mindset.

Create for yourself an environment where it's easy and natural for you to get your hands on the kind of material that will teach you to win in whatever you're trying to accomplish. And in addition to pursuing the right content, immerse yourself in listening to good examples of public speaking.

To win this media war, we recommend that you get on a monthly book and audio subscription, such as those offered by LIFE Leadership, so you won't have to rely on the possibility that you'll go to the bookstore each month, find something worth reading, and then read it.

Getting a subscription that sends you positive and excellent information each month makes it that much more likely that you'll *get* the material and also consistently listen to first-rate examples.

Listening to a lot of good speeches and speakers is one of the most effective ways to become a better speaker yourself.

## More Fishing

The knowledge you have is all you'll be able to use in your speeches, so if you want to be great, you need to be constantly filling yourself with great information.

Winning the media war is all about avoiding the kind of TV and magazine trash that will fill up your space with poor quality information and instead making a strong effort to put the good stuff in.

This is absolutely crucial to effective SPLASH speaking because, as we've said, if you don't *know* anything worthwhile, you probably won't *say* anything worthwhile—at least not very often.

So get on top of it! It's really not that hard to start getting the good stuff in, as Chris Brady and Orrin Woodward teach, and it will improve every aspect of your life. When you consistently fill your mind with quality information and examples, your happiness will grow along with your personal abilities and assets. And your instant access to good material will make your public speaking better.

Your family will be strengthened along with your business leadership. And as these things increase, so will your influence and skills as a SPLASH speaker.

To summarize, so far, we've learned the following:

1. You don't want to be a decent public speaker but rather a truly great SPLASH speaker, so that every speech changes the listeners and leaves long-term ripples of positive impact.
2. The first step of great (and even just good) public speaking is to deeply care about a cause that matters to you.
3. Don't just practice public speaking; practice giving speeches that really matter to you, speeches in which you can share your message. This kind of practice builds great public speakers.
4. Avoid trashy media, entertainment, and information that can water down your message. Instead, consistently fill up on top-quality ideas that will naturally pop into your mind when you are speaking to others.

# 4

## *Honestly, if everyone likes what you say, something is wrong with your message.*
### —ASHLEY ORMON

Once you've tackled the challenge of saying the right things to the right people and learning the right things from the right places, you're ready to face the sad part about even the most effective SPLASH speech: if you're really doing your job, you will make enemies.

It's easy to think that if people hate you or say mean things about you, you're doing something wrong. While people who go out of their way to do something wrong generally *do* experience this kind of negativity—as did Hitler, Stalin, and Mao—this alone is not proof of moral failure.

> *Criticism isn't something that comes to people for doing bad things; it's something that comes to people for attempting to do big things.*

The reality is that Joan of Arc, Socrates, Gandhi, and Jesus of Nazareth all experienced more than their fair share of negative feedback as well. In fact, they were all ultimately killed for what they believed and stood for.

Criticism isn't something that comes to people for doing *bad* things; it's something that comes to people for attempting to do *big* things. So if you aren't getting any criticism, you probably aren't making enough of a difference, and it's time to work harder and do more.

## Gauging and Changing

Criticism should be used as a way to gauge your success as a leader and a speaker, not as an alarm that says, "Change!" You shouldn't stop your work because someone didn't like it.

You should take that as a sign that you're making an impact! It should encourage you to keep doing what you're doing because it's starting to move things.

Of course, just as you take care to listen to the right mentors and find the right information when you're preparing your message, you should also consult them when you're checking and adjusting it.

If your message is offending and creating enemies of all the good guys, you should probably find out why. It's likely that you need to do some tweaking.

Watching *who* is doing the criticizing is the key to finding out whether you're having the kind of influence and impact you want. If the bad guys, losers, and looter-types are the ones who hate your message, you're doing something right.

On the other hand, if they all love you, while the great leaders, producers, and good guys think you're a villain, you probably have something to worry about.

## Which Side Are You On?

It comes down to this one question: Which side are you on? If you're working hard enough and truly making a difference, you'll also be making critics. What you have to decide is who you want as friends.

We bring this up early in this book because good speakers must first get their minds in the right place: (1) Know what you stand for, (2) take a stand for it, (3) don't waste time on distractions, (4) get your information and examples from the right people and places, and (5) join the battle for a cause that really matters to you!

Here's the main point: Any person who has done all five of these and continues doing them is going to have interesting content for speeches and will be asked to give lots of them. Plan on it! When you have something truly important to say, people will want to hear from you. But this requires a warrior-speaker mentality, a leader viewpoint!

On the other hand, if you aren't doing these five things, not many people will care much about what you have to say in a speech. Why should they? But when you stand for something meaningful, what you have to say will be worth listening to.

So which side are you on? Are you fighting for the right team or against it? Are your critics the right enemies, or aren't they?

That's the gauge of successful public speaking. In fact, it's the gauge of effective leadership and, ultimately, of effective action.

If you're making a difference and the bad guys criticize you, that's a good thing! It means not only that you're standing for the right things but that you're doing it so well that you've become a thorn in somebody's flesh. Keep it up!

People who try to be excellent public speakers without truly standing for something of value will never be more than mediocre or average speakers—even if their charm, preparation, and charismatic delivery are completely off the charts.

Speeches by such people won't hold a candle to simple honesty and passion from someone who really cares and has taken a stand for a cause that deeply matters.

The first may receive awards or praise for his or her speeches, but the second will leave audiences touched, moved, and forever changed. When people leave the first speech, they'll say, "Wasn't that speaker amazing? Wow!" When they leave the second, they'll say, "I'm going to change myself, starting now." And they will.

That is what the **S** in SPLASH stands for: "**S**ay Something That Matters!" We'll learn more about how to say it effectively later, but without this first step, nobody will ever be a truly great speaker.

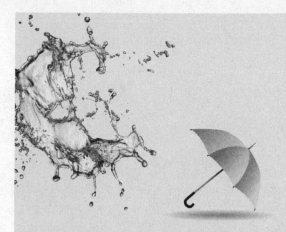

# SPLASH Zone!

1. Know what you stand for.

2. Take a real stand for your cause, and learn to promote it through public speaking.

3. Don't waste time on distractions.

4. Get your information, media, and examples from the right people and places.

5. Listen to feedback from the right people and improve your speaking as you learn from them. Be happy when the bad guys are your critics; this means you're making a real difference.

# Prepare the Speaker, Not Just the Speech

*All things are ready, if our mind be so.*
—William Shakespeare

# 5

## *It usually takes me more than three weeks to prepare a good impromptu speech.*

—MARK TWAIN

This quotation from Mark Twain is brilliant because, although he may have said it simply for shock or entertainment value, it expresses an often misunderstood rule of speaking and speech preparation, the **P** in SPLASH: "**P**repare the *Speaker*, Not Just the Speech."

> *While individual speech preparation is important, the preparation that goes into the speaker is much more significant.*

While individual speech preparation is important, the preparation that goes into the speaker personally is much more significant.

Of course, all the chapters so far have discussed vital ways any truly effective public speaker needs to prepare. But there are a number of other principles of good SPLASH speaking.

### Informal or Impromptu

For one thing, there are often occasions in a leader's life when he or she will be called upon to give an informal and sometimes even an impromptu speech. If you only focus on preparing speeches and never truly prepare yourself as a speaker, you're almost certain to fall short on these occasions.

This is sad because these speeches are often the most important and impactful talks a speaker can ever give, specifically because they flow naturally in the moment based on the needs and readiness of the audience.

The opportunities that come suddenly to speak well (or poorly, as the case may be) are times when the audience—though often quite a bit smaller than a more formal one—is in deep need of some specific lesson, idea, or information and is therefore ready to drink it up and really apply it.

Such audience readiness is rare and precious. If your only option when such an opportunity arises is a mediocre or poor speech, you're seriously lacking in SPLASHability.

## Reading Your Audience

Another reason that preparing the speaker is so vitally important is that sometimes the speech you've prepared is simply not the best one for the audience you've gathered.

No matter how hard you study your demographic and advertise to a certain crowd, it's impossible to know exactly who your audience will be until you're actually speaking to them—even if you got exactly the people you invited.

As a result, someone who only prepares speeches will have much less flexibility and will be less able to deliver the talk that will have the greatest impact on the audience that actually shows up.

In contrast, well-prepared *speakers* will be able to utilize any speech preparation they have done, even as they adapt to the audience they are with at the time. Such speakers will be able to rely on their preparation for this particular speech as well as any others they have given, those they have heard, and everything they have read.

They'll be able to stick to the plan or improvise in meaningful and effective ways—or both if they choose.

## But *Do* Prepare

Of course, we're not saying you should plan to simply read a lot and then improvise every speech from square one—far from it. Do prepare. However, while most people who gear up to give a speech recognize the importance of preparing *that* speech, speakers often forget or don't even think about the significant value of preparing themselves as speakers before each event.

As you're preparing each individual speech, you should take special care to consider how you can be preparing yourself to be a great speaker in the long term. Just thinking about it during your "speech preparations" will have a surprisingly big effect on your "speaker preparation."

By preparing both speech *and* speaker, you'll be equipping yourself for greater success, regardless of any bumps, surprises, or unexpected happenings that arise while you're speaking. And you'll be practicing real leadership.

In addition, you'll be more ready for the unexpected things that come when you didn't think you *would* be speaking or that change from what you expected at an event.

But *how* do you "prepare the speaker"? We'll discuss this in the next three chapters.

# 6

## *If you don't know what you want to achieve in your presentation, your audience never will.*

—HARVEY DIAMOND

One of the main reasons that knowing your cause and why it matters to you is such a critical step in effective SPLASH speaking is that it's also the first step to preparing yourself as a speaker.

Since we've already discussed this principle in depth, we'll let it go with one final reminder: If you don't have something worthwhile to say, you're not ready to speak. On the flip side, if you *do* have an important message, you'll at least have a base for impromptu and informal speaking as well as for necessary course correction in your well-prepared speeches.

If you know the big picture, you can develop and adjust it for any situation that comes along. In this way, having a cause is crucial to quality preparation.

If you haven't paid the price to know what you stand for, you may as well stop standing because all you're doing is getting tired legs. This tends to waste your time and that of your audience as well.

## Get the Big Picture, Every Single Time

Now that you know your overall big picture (what you stand for, etc.), you're prepared in general to be a speaker. But the real power of this principle comes into play when you apply this *speaker* preparation to each individual *speech* preparation.

You know how to find your cause and why it matters, so now you can use the technique to prepare yourself as a speaker for each speech. In reality, before you can be an effective speaker, you have to clearly define what "effective" looks like to you.

> *Until you know what you're shooting at, it's extremely difficult to aim well, and you'll have a very hard time getting the audience to follow your line of fire.*

Until you know what you're shooting at, it's extremely difficult to aim well, and you'll have a very hard time getting the audience to follow your line of fire.

Just as knowing your life mission, purpose, or cause helps you decide which speaking engagements you should accept, knowing your "speech cause" for an upcoming talk will help you decide which stories to tell, which impressions to follow, which methods to use, and so on.

If you know what your purpose is, you can target your work and preparation toward that, so you won't waste opportunities to really further your cause.

## Here's How It Works

Visualize yourself *after* the speech, and notice every point that contributed to the effectiveness or "success" of your presentation. How did you speak, and what were you wearing? What visuals did you use, if any? How did you open and close? How did you interact with the audience? How were they *changed* by the time you finished?

Picture all of these in your mind before you speak. And once you know how you want the audience members to be changed after you speak, adjust your speech to this goal.

Popular speaker and author Terri Brady taught:

> We often think that "prepared" means that we have a Point A and a Point B and a Point C, but there's so much more to it than that.
>
> A good speaker compels people to be different by the time they leave. It's not just about talking and filling the air with words. But when people leave, are they different than when they first heard you speak? Are they *different*? Are they challenged to change?

In essence, you have to define what impact you had on the audience. Once you know what your success looks like and can visualize it in your mind (before you start), it's far easier to prepare prior to your speech and to adapt toward it when you're onstage.

## The Right Nos and the Right Yeses

Once you have a big-picture goal for every speech and are in the habit of developing a macro and micro vision for each one, your speaking effectiveness will start to grow exponentially. This works!

> *Envision what you want before you speak, including how you want your listeners to be changed, and then do whatever is helpful in adapting your speech to that goal.*

As you begin to act in a focused and intentional way toward a specific and clearly defined goal of success, you'll be able to recognize and discard what doesn't help you and embrace what does.

Again, you'll be able to do this as you visualize before the talk and also as needed onstage while you're speaking. The power of this micro plan is enormous!

To make it even clearer, envision what you want before you speak, including how you want your listeners to be changed, and then do whatever is helpful in adapting your speech to that goal.

Do this with every speech.

# 7

## *A speaker should approach his preparation not by what he wants to say, but by what he wants to learn.*

—TODD STOCKER

When it comes to targeted speaking and intentional impact, it's vital for each speaker to remember the importance of being a truly hungry student. In reality, we're all students—or we should be—and the speaker who is still learning will always have the most to teach.

A speaker who is thinking big and important ideas is preparing to be an excellent SPLASH speaker! This is much deeper than merely outlining and preparing a speech.

> *The speaker who is still learning will always have the most to teach.*

A great way to do this is to follow the excellent advice of Todd Stocker and prepare based on your own needs, not just those of your intended audience(s).

For example, have you ever heard a talk where the speaker said, "When I sat down to prepare this speech, I thought I knew what I was talking about. But by the end, I realized that I needed this as much as anyone"? While this isn't always the most effective way to present yourself as a speaker, it *is* one of the most effective ways to *treat* yourself as a speaker, especially before the speech.

**A Mile in Their Shoes**

To effectively prepare yourself as a speaker as you plan and get ready for each individual speech, think about what you need to learn from the topic.

While you probably shouldn't be lecturing people in areas where you have no results yourself, you should be giving yourself constant reminders and refresher courses on your areas of passion and expertise because if you don't, you'll quickly get outdated.

> *One of the most powerful tools of great public speaking is personal passion.*

As we'll discuss in greater depth later on, one of the most powerful tools of great public speaking is personal passion. What are you passionate about? How are you conveying that to your audience?

If you're using speech preparation to teach yourself the new and exciting aspects of whatever it is you're speaking about, your passion for your topic—and for continued learning—will be more likely to show up in your speeches in a way that the audience will *feel*.

As you start to prepare for your speech, pretend that you're the audience for a little while, and get yourself excited about the new information and ideas you're learning! Not only will this be more fun for you and make you a better person and leader, but it will also improve your speeches. Your passion for your topic and for learning needs to be contagious.

Of course, in order for this to work, you can't spend the *whole* preparation time thinking purely about what you can get out of your speech. Eventually, you need to think about the audience you will be speaking to.

## Don't Throw Steaks at the Baby!

Terri Brady reminds us that, while we should always be excited and learning new things about our speaking topics, we shouldn't walk out onstage and spout everything new we've learned. Usually, the audience members will have less expertise in the subject matter than you do; that's why you're the speaker instead of them.

And just because you're at the "steak" level doesn't mean you should be throwing steak at people who still need baby food.

Start your speaker preparation by learning fresh and interesting stuff yourself and increasing your own level of fitness to present the topic. Eat your steak dinner. But when you're finished, you need to break it all down in such a way that it will have the right impact on the audience your speech is going to influence.

By including both steak and baby food in your preparation, you'll ensure that your speech is not only the best you have to offer but also the best for the audience. Do your homework before a talk so you can address it in as many ways and levels as needed. Then deliver your message in the way your specific audience will get the most from it.

# 8

## *Ninety percent of how well the talk will go is determined before the speaker steps on the platform.*

—SOMERS WHITE

Despite all this focus on speaker preparation, it's important that you don't neglect the power and significance of actually preparing your speeches. There's a reason this section of the book isn't called "Prepare the Speaker, Never the Speech" or even "Prepare the Speaker, Not the Speech."

The **P** principle of SPLASH speaking is "**P**repare the Speaker, Not *Just* the Speech." To put it bluntly, you almost certainly should prepare most of your speeches. In fact, you should prepare them really well because if you don't, they'll probably suffer for it.

One very powerful technique for speech preparation is to write your speech out word for word. This method is often misunderstood and generally misused, but let's talk about how it can make a world of difference in your public speaking when it is used correctly.

### You Wouldn't Want to Miss Something

For one thing, writing out your speech helps you coherently organize your thoughts and ideas. By doing this, you are able to make mental and literal notes of all the most important points you want to make and plan for the most effective ways to express and illustrate them.

One of the main difficulties beginning speakers face is an apparent inability to cover everything that matters. Even if they have a good set of supporting facts, stories, analogies, and metaphors to use, they rarely remember them at every useful point of their presentation.

What this sometimes looks like is a random, incoherent, and poorly delivered jumble of ideas that rarely comes together in a way that works for a large portion of the audience.

By first planning and then writing out the entire speech, you effectively eliminate this piecemeal aspect. And you prepare yourself to give a talk that makes sense, supports itself well, and leaves the audience to focus on the message instead of just trying to keep up with what on earth you are saying.

## Why Go Shallow?

If you make yourself write out your speech before you deliver it, you'll probably end up developing it much more than if you only made a simple outline and then tried to wing the rest.

By taking the time to write it all out, you'll be able to see holes in your speech that would otherwise go unnoticed and unattended. This process makes the gaps obvious, so all you have to do is go in and fill them up.

You know your cause and message already, and hope-fully you know your audience, so it should be a simple matter of fitting the two together.

Doing this generally has the excellent effect of making your speech both deeper and more relatable, which is pretty awesome! Sadly, people too often worry that making themselves more relatable means making them-selves more shallow. But in the realm of ideas, this just isn't so.

Being relatable is a good thing because if you aren't relatable, you probably aren't influencing anyone. But if the people you're trying to relate to are too shallow to appreciate depth and a great cause, you should probably look back to the first section of this book and put your focus on influencing different people or advancing a different cause.

Actually, it may just be that you aren't doing the work required to relate to them—that they're not shallow at all but that your preparation is lacking.

## It's All about the Transfer

Effective writing and effective speaking aren't the same, but they are definitely based on the same principles, the primary foundation of both being good communication. A writer and a speaker both seek to communicate with their audience in very specific ways—not just to make them understand, but rather to help them understand *and* transfer a feeling.

Understanding the connection between these two powerful forms of communication also helps clarify why writing out your speech can make it better, clearer, and more capable of truly and positively shifting the minds and hearts of the audience receiving it.

This is not to say that every good writer will automatically be able to stand up and give a powerful speech that moves

> *Help them understand and transfer a feeling.*

the crowd to their feet and sends them running toward a new and brighter future (even if his or her *writings* do just that).

However, one of the most valuable ways a person can develop as a speaker is to practice the art of writing.

Writing and speaking are the same in that they are about learning and organization, deepening and strengthening your ideas, and then sharing them with others in a way that makes them want to change and improve.

After learning to do this in writing, it's a lot easier for most people to do the same thing in a speech. In this way, the act of writing your speech is an excellent way to practice for public speaking.

Just as learning a second language usually makes it easier to learn a third, and learning the second and the third will make the fourth even easier, learning to write will make learning to speak effectively more manageable. And constant practice of both will strengthen each.

## Don't Be Fooled

Writing out your speech is a great way to prepare but reading it is not usually a good way to actually give the speech! This is very important.

After reading (to fill your head with ideas in the first place), writing is one of the best preparations for effective speaking. Of course, if all you ever do is sit around writing speeches and never giving them, or reading speeches and never *speaking*, you'll never create real SPLASHes as a speaker.

But if you master the art of writing speeches and take the time to organize and deepen each talk by writing it out well, you will likely ease the jump from listener to speaker.

As mentioned, the problem with writing out your speech is that once you have done this, you'll probably be tempted to read it aloud to the audience. This is almost always a bad idea.

Don't read your speech. But do write it out. Then, once the written version is just how you want it, put it in a file and don't even take it with you to the speaking event. Speak from the heart, or use an outline, but don't just read to the audience.

> *Writing out the speech is about preparing the speaker, not the speech. This distinction is critical.*

Writing out the speech is about preparing the speaker, not the speech. This distinction is critical. If this practice was about preparing the speech, you could just read it to the audience. But since it is about preparing the speaker, you can gain a great deal by writing it out and then leaving it backstage.

Speakers who have written a speech well and then put it away somewhere are nearly always able to deliver the message more effectively! They don't say exactly what's on the paper; in fact, they say it better!

Many advanced speakers reach the point where they can skip this step because they do the same thing by thinking about the words they're going to say over and over in the weeks or days leading up to the speech.

But for most beginning speakers, writing out the speech can help clarify and refine the message and delivery. Again, the key is to write it, write it well, and then put it away!

Note that you can do the same thing with an outline. Write it out, read it over twice a day for a week before your speech, and then leave it at home or backstage and speak from the heart! Or, since it's just an outline, you can use it during the speech to keep yourself on target, but make sure you spend most of the time looking in the eyes of the audience members, not down at your notes!

# 9

## *I never let practical considerations clutter my youthful dreams.*
### —ROY CHAPMAN ANDREWS

The above quotation teaches a valuable principle that has a powerful application when it comes to public speaking. It's vital that you don't limit your dreaming by the type of depressed downerism that the world has dubbed "realism." That's why we've spent so much time emphasizing the significance and power of choosing a cause and dedicating your life to it. However, there is an important time and place for practical considerations, and if you don't deal with them effectively, you *will* be limiting your dreams, as well as your ability to achieve them, by refusing to live in a world that truly is real. So once you've ignored the modern, pessimistic realism long enough to build a vision of your success, it's time to face head-on the actual realities of your situation.

Here is a list of practical considerations that, if properly dealt with, will improve your speaking ability immensely.

## Appearance

One important aspect of presentation in public speaking, but also in any situation where you're dealing with people, is dress and appearance.

As with most aspects of effective SPLASH speaking, appropriate dress is all about knowing your audience and dressing in the manner that best fits the needs of those people. The easiest and simplest way to do this is to ask what the audience will be wearing and then shoot to be one notch above them. This makes you relatable, while simultaneously presenting you as an authority figure— someone they should actually listen to.

There's really no black-and-white explanation of what you should wear to give a speech; just make sure it is appropriate for your venue and audience.

The other appearance essential involves your face: Smile! Most of us think we're smiling all the time, especially onstage. But when we really look into this, it's almost shocking how few of us do enough of it. So make a point of being the one wearing a big smile!

## Eliminate Distracting Mannerisms and Language

Frequent use of phrases, words, and fillers such as "you know," "umm," or "like" often tends to distract your audience in a negative way, so pace yourself and make sure you break these habits as early as possible.

In fact, if you're using too many buzzwords or figures of speech in general, you might want to cut down on them. These are not absolute evils, but they can detract from your performance because your audience can become fixated on them and stop listening to your actual point.

If your audience is keeping an "umm" tally, they probably aren't really getting your message. And audience members almost never come away with the desired change in such a situation.

Chewing gum and drinking water every three seconds clearly fit into this category. So leave the gum backstage, and make a point of only drinking when your voice needs it—or not at all, if possible.

Repetitive gestures, pacing, and other sidetracking motions or actions can also divert attention from your point to your person, so watch yourself on these as well. Of course, you should move around a little as you speak, if the venue allows, but make sure your movements are adding to your message rather than taking away from it. Make any motions and gestures relevant and meaningful.

A really valuable way to keep track of these things for future reference is to videotape your speeches so you can watch them later and critique yourself for specific pointers and increased learning.

## Find Your Own Special Style or Unique Speaking Brand

Listen and learn from as many great speakers as possible, but eventually, you'll want to be your own person. It's important to differentiate between learning from others who've gained success and just plain being unoriginal.

Create a signature style and make yourself memorable through it. Make sure your "style" isn't negativity, arrogance, or false humility. Always be more positive than not. And, as Chris Brady says, "Always follow the rules of civility."

Also, make a point of giving proper credit to those you quote or reference and give honor and edification to the right people in a way that's meaningful to your audience. It's probably best if you *don't* use yourself as the "perfect example" to illustrate your points. Don't tell the audience how awesome you were at something last week. It only makes you seem smug or arrogant.

### *You* Follow the Clock, but *They* Should Forget It

Try to avoid repeated references to how much time you have left, how far over you are, and anything else that has to do with the clock. Your audience should wonder how the time passed so quickly when your speech ends, but if you're constantly mentioning it, they'll start wondering how soon you'll be done rather than listening to what you're trying to say.

Also, don't try to tell them what you're going to tell them all at once at the beginning of your speech. Just launch right into it. When you give them an overview at the beginning, it usually just makes them zone out.

Get them interested in the content itself as soon as possible, so you don't waste their time or yours with endless droning about the future message you've got planned for them.

### Be Practical, but Move On

Now that we've got these quick pointers down, watch yourself and find out which ones are for you. Then use them!

Again, these aren't the most important part of your success as a SPLASH speaker, but they will make a definite, positive difference in your impact.

The idea is to drop anything that distracts from your real point and message so that you and the audience can connect on a deep level, without getting caught up on tangents of appearance, weirdness, or other distractions. As you do this, your impact as a speaker will grow exponentially.

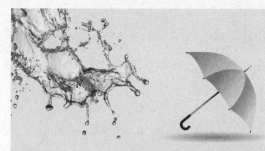

# SPLASH Zone!

1. Know what you stand for.

2. Take a real stand for your cause, and learn to promote it through public speaking.

3. Don't waste time on distractions.

4. Get your information, media, and examples from the right people and places.

5. Listen to feedback from the right people and improve your speaking as you learn from them. Be happy when the bad guys are your critics; this means you're making a real difference.

6. Prepare the speaker (you) for every speech by knowing how you want the audience to be changed when you finish speaking.

7. Before every speech, visualize how the audience will respond and what they'll do after they go home, and change your speech as needed to obtain this goal.

8. Learn something new and interesting about the topic before every speech.

9. If you are a beginning speaker, try writing out your talk in detail, then making an outline, and then throwing it all away before you go onstage. This process will help you prepare the speaker and not just the speech!

10. Make a point of dealing with the little, practical considerations that could distract your audience from your message.

# Leave It All Backstage

*If we never had the courage to take a leap of faith,
we'd be cheating God out of a chance to mount us up
with wings like eagles and watch us soar.*
—Jen Stephens

# 10

## *Pray as though everything depended on God. Work as though everything depended on you.*

—Saint Augustine

This concept taught by Saint Augustine is one of the very best tips ever written about public speaking.

Now that you've planned out every little piece of your speech, down to writing the words you want to share, it's time to make a nice stack of all your notes and plans and leave them at home or somewhere offstage where the audience can't see them.

Leave all your preparations behind, walk out onstage, take stock of your audience, and deliver a fantastic speech.

If you have limited experience with public speaking, you may have been surprised at the suggestion to write out your entire talk. Indeed, if you've ever heard a speech that was delivered entirely by reading from a page, you know that it isn't the most effective way to inspire an audience. Not at all.

In fact, it's one of the most boring deliveries possible. And if your audience is bored, they probably aren't listening very closely; and if they're not listening, they certainly aren't going to change much—except maybe their minds about coming to hear you speak.

As we've said, writing your speech is a great preparatory tool, but a terrible delivery method. (The one exception is when you pass out copies of the speech because you want people to take it home and reread it. But this is usually reserved for experienced speakers, and most of them still end up straying from reading the speech at some point in their delivery.) So once you've prepared down to the commas and periods, you should scrap the whole thing and walk out onstage with nothing but your heart.

## Why You've Gotta Do *Both*

In other words, work as if your entire success depends on the perfection of your written speech, and then speak as though it all depends on you winging it and speaking from your heart. Ultimately, both can be true.

Again, note that many experienced speakers don't do this anymore, so they may tell you it isn't all that beneficial. But if they take the time to remember how they became great speakers, most of them will recall that this process really did help them.

The best speeches are those that incorporate a perfect balance of deep preparation

> *The best speeches are those that incorporate a perfect balance of deep preparation and openly inspired improvisation.*

and openly inspired improvisation. You'll probably use

quite a bit of your prepared content in most of your speeches; that's great! That's why you prepared. But you should also be open to new ideas or directions you feel inspired to speak about when you're in front of the audience. Remember, your purpose is to help and move them, not to check off the items on your outline.

Sometimes, on the other hand, you'll end up giving a totally new and unanticipated talk, based on what the audience really needs. This is fantastic. It's the reason you prepared yourself as a speaker instead of relying solely on your speech notes.

It's okay to bring a list of points you want to share or a quotation you want to read. Reading a quote to the audience is fine, as long as it is a short contribution and doesn't take over your whole speech.

The ability to combine your intentions with the audience's needs is a huge difference between mediocre or good speakers and great, truly effective SPLASH speakers.

Understanding and applying this principle takes work and practice, but it is definitely worth it. Mastering it will significantly increase your level of influence as a public speaker.

# 11

## *Self-consciousness kills communication.*
### —RICK STEVES

Top leader and fantastic public speaker Chris Brady teaches about the importance of not taking your- self too lightly while simultaneously not taking yourself too seriously either. This is *excellent* counsel.

Keeping the right perspective will enable you to deliver a meaningful message that actually makes its way into the hearts and minds of the people you're trying to help. Speaking is both a responsibility and a privilege. When you get up in front of an audience, all those people are relying on you to make it a success.

### Responsibility and Privilege

Every member of the audience came to hear what you have to say, and they sacrificed their time (and probably more) to do so. You have a responsibility to make it worth their time and sacrifice.

Also, whoever set up the event probably spent dozens, and sometimes even hundreds, of hours to make it a reality, and they're counting on you to make it good.

Speaking is also a huge privilege. There aren't many places where you can get up and share your deepest passions, thoughts, and ideas with so many people at once and have many or even all of them really listening and waiting to change their lives in response.

This responsibility and privilege of public speaking should keep you from taking it too lightly. Instead, give each speech your focused consideration and preparation.

## Honor

On the other hand, speaking isn't just a responsibility and a privilege. It's also an honor, and usually one based on merit. As Brady puts it, whoever asked you to speak to their crowd probably didn't select you because they liked your haircut or thought your tie would look good with their backdrops. (And if they did, you should probably think twice about taking the speaking engagement.) For some reason, they thought you had something important to give to their people, and they wanted more than a cardboard cutout. They wanted your voice, your mind, your insights, your personality, your style. They wanted *you*.

So be honored that you were chosen, but don't let it go to your head. Don't allow the event to become about you. If you do, you're taking yourself too seriously. When you do this, you're being both selfish and unreasonable. You're probably standing onstage worrying about how you look, what they think of you, or whether you have spinach in your teeth.

In short, if you're thinking about yourself the whole time, you're not thinking about the audience. And, as Chris Brady says, "They're the ones you're here to serve."

If you're not thinking about the audience because you're taking yourself too seriously, then you usually aren't making those valuable and even vital connections that allow you to deliver a truly impactful SPLASH speech.

## The Right Balance

Being a little bit jittery or nervous is okay, Brady says, if you teach those butterflies to fly in formation because that will turn into adrenaline, which will help you perform better. But don't lose sight of who really matters, and it's *not* you.

Whoever invited you there was clearly comfortable with your merits as a speaker; don't prove them wrong by doing their job interview for them onstage. There's no point in trying to decide if you're worthy of the honor of speaking when you're already onstage! The time for self-consciousness is long past; now it's time to deliver.

So if you find yourself onstage worrying about anything other than your message and the audience who needs to receive it, stop it! Focus in on the present and your purpose in speaking. Emphasize what you stand for! Think about the audience.

> *The time for self-consciousness is long past; now it's time to deliver.*

## The Cure

Popular speaker Orrin Woodward teaches that the cure for self-consciousness is preparation. He said, "The more you prepare, the less you'll be thinking about yourself." Woodward himself is an excellent example of the value of preparation. In his early days as a speaker and business leader, he would often show up to an event two hours early so he could go over his speech notes at the venue. In doing this, he was building his confidence through preparation.

So as we've already discussed, make sure you give yourself enough real preparation before you step out onstage so that you'll be able to forget about yourself, and even your preparation, and really focus on your audience and your message.

> *"The more you prepare, the less you'll be thinking about yourself."*
> —Orrin Woodward

Know who you are, who you're talking to, and what you need to say so you don't have to worry about any of those things onstage. You'll be able to just *communicate.* Communication is the first goal, and if you aren't communicating, you're definitely not inspiring anyone to change in the ways they need.

# 12

## *Ideas come from everything.*
### —ALFRED HITCHCOCK

It is extremely important that as you're speaking, you share ideas that will improve the effectiveness of your presentation, no matter where those ideas come from. You never know when you're going to be miraculously hit with the exact burst of inspiration that will make your speech a true success.

Often the things that suddenly pop into your mind won't be very surprising at all, since they'll be related to the plan or outline you spent hours and hours preparing. But when this isn't the case, be thankful that you somehow managed to come up with something important that you had previously missed. Don't dismiss a great idea simply because it wasn't in your original plan. After all, this is one of the main reasons you didn't bring your written-out speech onstage with you.

### Leave It All Backstage

The idea is to leave all of that stuff backstage and speak from your heart, so if your heart suggests something new right when you happen to need it, great! Everything is working beautifully, and your speech will be that much better if you listen and apply those little spur-of-the-moment epiphanies or insights.

Of course, make sure they are appropriate and helpful, but go with them if they'll improve your message.

Perhaps as you make eye contact with a member of your audience, hear the tone of the audience's laughter, or feel the energy in the room, some old poem, quotation, story, example, or thought will present itself, seemingly out of nowhere. This is a wonderful occurrence that should make you very happy. It could mean that you're about to say something this particular audience really needs at this precise moment. And in turn, that means you'll be making your speech truly meaningful and impactful.

## Helping Them to Help You Help Them

This principle presents a very intriguing dilemma with a surprising and fascinating solution. The most effective public speakers, as you know very well by now, stand for something that really matters to them and to the world. This means they have much to gain from success and much to lose in failure. Knowing this, they choose their speaking engagements based on what will get them—and others—closer to their ultimate reward.

In this way, the best speakers are very self-centered, even if the "self" refers to a deep and mature cause instead of a desire that is frivolous or just plain greedy. Another way to say this is that they are very focused.

On the other hand, the best public speakers, the ones who really make a SPLASH, are also the ones who dedicate their lives to true service. They do everything they can to help others improve their lives and situations and ultimately make the world a much better place.

This adds a level of depth and an interesting dynamic to the whole picture. Luckily, the classical economist Adam Smith comes to the rescue!

## The Invisible Hand

Smith taught the idea of the "Invisible Hand," which basically means that as government leaves the economy alone to do its own thing, the economy will act in a clearly visible and productive pattern, as though it were controlled by an invisible hand.

What does this stealthy power do? It's all about individual self-interest and how it ultimately benefits society as a whole. Smith taught that as people act in their own self-interest, competing in a free-market economy, society will see significant progress and prosperity, and everyone will be helped by *any*one's efforts to improve things for themselves.

How is that the answer we've been waiting for? Anything honest, good, and valuable that you do to help yourself will ultimately help everyone around you, and vice versa. (Obviously, if you're lying, cheating, or stealing, the principle doesn't work the same.)

So when you are genuinely doing good, excellent things to help others—as long as they're the right things—you'll also help yourself, and doing the right things to further *your* cause will also help everyone around you. This principle, originally a principle of good economics, has an important place in public speaking.

## Translation

When you can translate your needs and your message into effective answers for the needs of your audience members, you've not only won a significant battle for your cause but also helped them defeat a major foe as well. As we'll discuss in depth in the following section, your speech is all about the unification of your cause and your audience.

When you really help the listeners with their challenges and obstacles by showing them that a meaningful cause is the answer to all their problems, everybody comes out a winner!

So listen to the ideas that come from "all over the place" as you're speaking. Whether they're inspired by the lighting in the room, the reaction of the crowd, the way you sort of tripped as you walked out, or anything else, pay attention to these thoughts that strike you during your talk. Many of them can be incredibly important and powerful, and they can help make your speech a brilliant success.

# 13

## *Don't spread negativity; that stuff is contagious and ruins us.*

—JOSHUA NEIK

Another helpful way to apply the "Leave It All Backstage" principle is the anti-negativity stun gun. Of course, this secret weapon is symbolic, not literal. We don't think shooting yourself with any real weapon will help you deliver your best speeches. But if you master the use of this hidden treasure, you'll be tackling one of the biggest challenges to effective public speaking.

Before you go onstage, shoot yourself with this figurative gun and forget all the negative things that are going on back there. That way, all you take with you into the spotlight is your positivity, your vision, your personal preparation, your hope, and your will to succeed!

### Forgive or Forget

If you want to be truly effective in your speech, leave your bad attitude, annoyances, pet peeves, the bad day you are having, and every other negative behind you, and stay focused on the message you're there to deliver. Disney University actually takes this a step further, teaching that whatever is *backstage* will end up *onstage,* so make sure everything is smooth behind the scenes.

While this isn't always possible, you certainly should make a point of resolving anything and everything you can before you walk out in front of the crowd. This will make it much easier for you to stay focused and to perform in a way that will have a meaningful impact on your audience. It will also make it easier for you to stay happy and dedicated to whatever task you should be focusing on at any given moment.

That said, every top speaker has had to learn to walk out onstage and deliver a talk even though terrible or worrisome things are happening "in the background."

### "Take Five"

Taking a few minutes to review your speech vision and your overall purpose as a speaker right before you go onstage is an excellent way to start the process of leaving your negatives behind. Especially if you've taken measures to resolve the easy fixes, remembering why *this* particular speech matters will help you come back to the present and stay there.

### What Does and Does *Not* Work

If you want your talk to be successful, you have to be 100 percent present as a speaker. You need to be aware of the flow of your speech and the reacting energy of the audience, and then you can make sure to keep them connected in the right ways.

This doesn't work if you're thinking about other problems or concerns. In fact, the only time it *does* work is when you know what you want out of the speech, what the audience needs from it, and how to bring the two together.

Remembering this goal and how it fits into your big-picture cause is the first step to forgetting your woes.

Once that's done, you just have to remember it every time the worries or problems start to sneak into your thoughts. Anytime negatives introduce themselves into your mind, rebuff them with your purpose.

## Prepare for Overwhelming Positives

You'll never really know beforehand what challenges you will face when you actually deliver your speech, so make sure that in your preparation time, you make your speech vision strong enough and clear enough that it *matters* enough to push the bad stuff out of the way so you can give a winning speech.

The second part to the Neik quote that gives this chapter its name reads, "The good news is, positivity can also be contagious, and it lifts us."

If you know what you're about and take great care to make it bigger and better and more persuasive than anything the world throws at you, you can use your grounded positives to effectively dismiss any negatives that come.

Learning to leave these things behind when you go to change the world will make a huge difference in your ability to create a real and powerful SPLASH.

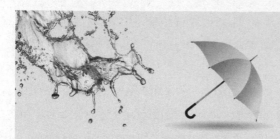

# SPLASH Zone!

1. Know what you stand for.

2. Take a real stand for your cause, and learn to promote it through public speaking.

3. Don't waste time on distractions.

4. Get your information, media, and examples from the right people and places.

5. Listen to feedback from the right people and improve your speaking as you learn from them. Be happy when the bad guys are your critics; this means you're making a real difference.

6. Prepare the speaker (you) for every speech by knowing how you want the audience to be changed when you finish speaking.

7. Before every speech, visualize how the audience will respond and what they'll do after they go home, and change your speech as needed to obtain this goal.

8. Learn something new and interesting about the topic before every speech.

9. If you are a beginning speaker, try writing out your talk in detail, then making an outline, and then throwing it all away before you go onstage. This process will help you prepare the speaker and not just the speech!

10. Make a point of dealing with the little, practical considerations that could distract your audience from your message.

11. Be centered on who you are and what you have to offer before you ever walk onstage. Remember that speaking is a privilege, a responsibility, and an honor, so focus on your purpose there, not your insecurities.

12. Be open to new thoughts and ideas that come to you as you're speaking; these are often the best segments of your talk.

13. Leave negatives and challenges backstage by creating a clear, strong vision and following it. Replace worries or concerns with a renewed focus on your speech's purpose.

# Audience Is Everything

*I made mistakes in drama. I thought drama was when actors cried. But drama is when the audience cries.*
—Frank Capra

# 14

## *Just because it's interesting to you doesn't mean it's interesting.*

—TIM MARKS

The book *Mentoring Matters* shares a very important idea: "The main difference between a good public speaker and a great public speaker is her ability to read an audience and adapt her speech in real time to fit its needs."

While everything you will learn in this book can be helpful, and some are even crucial, this one thing will ultimately make or break you as a speaker. If you can't connect with an audience, you will never affect them from the stage, no matter how great and essential your cause is to the future success and happiness of the universe. That's the simple truth of the matter. The end.

So how do you connect with your audience and escape an early end to an unsuccessful speaking career?

### Listen to Tim

First of all, the title quote of this chapter is a big clue. As we learn from Tim Marks, you can't just assume that your passion for a topic is shared by everyone in your audience. You have to inspire them. That's your job as a speaker.

As Claude Hamilton teaches, it's not so much what the audience members remember after a speech; it's the feelings they can't ever forget! Such feelings are life-altering, like a huge SPLASH you remember for the rest of your life.

Have you ever been on a boat or ferry and seen a whale jumping in the ocean? Most people have seen this on television or in a movie, and it is pretty spectacular. In fact, you're probably picturing the scene from TV right now as you read this.

But if you've seen this in real life, you are no doubt having strong feelings as well! Your memory of this makes you smile, shake your head, and say, "Wow! That was so incredible! I'll never, ever forget it!"

That's the power of SPLASH.

> *It's not so much what the audience members remember after a speech; it's the feelings they can't ever forget!*

That said, probably your first goal when you step onstage is to get the audience interested in you. Once they're interested in *you*, then they're interested in what you have to say. From there, it's a pretty simple process to get them excited about what you're excited about.

Now you can't do this in a self-conscious or conceited way, but if they're not interested in you, they probably won't care what you have to say.

## Balance Knowing with Caring

John C. Maxwell said it really well when he wrote, "People don't care how much you know until they know how much you care." This can be taken in a few ways.

First of all, it could mean that people don't care about your opinions until they know that you care about them personally. This is really important because as a speaker, you want your audience to trust you and feel that your advice is really directed toward their best interest. If the audience members don't feel like they matter to you, they're pretty unlikely to want to listen to your advice. After all, to them, you're just a greedy, smooth-talking salesperson—unless they know how much you care about them and want to help them improve their lives.

A second way this quote could be understood is that people don't care about what you have to say unless *you* do. If you sound bored by your topic, why would they be pumped to hear about it? They wouldn't. This is important for speakers to remember and pay attention to as they speak. It would be unfortunate to distract your audience from your message with your own boredom, monotony, or distraction.

## Don't Scream Their Ears Off!

Chris Brady reminds us how important it is *not* to be the kind of one-dimensional speaker who talks in the same voice with the same volume or expression throughout the whole speech. When you do this, you lose all the power of pauses, quiet moments, loud and intense moments, and so on.

Brady rightly teaches speakers to vary their voice, intensity, and expressions. If your whole speech is loud and intense, you'll leave with a hoarse voice, and even though the crowd might be excited at the time, they will probably leave with a headache and a desire to avoid all future events with your name on the program.

Yet there is certainly a time and a place to get loud in speeches. Chris Brady himself is a great example of this. He sometimes raises his voice to the point of almost yelling in his speeches, but it hasn't stopped anyone from wanting to hear him speak or from going home afterward truly changed and improved. This is because he knows when to talk loudly and when to talk quietly. He uses variety. Along with changing the intensity, he also uses long pauses, and at times, he speaks very softly so the audience has to lean in to hear him. He also strategically moderates the speed of his speech. Sometimes he talks faster than most people comfortably can, yet it has power to the listener since he doesn't *always* do it.

If you watch, you'll notice that all great speakers do these things. The idea here is to change it up. Be personal and real. If you deliver your whole speech from one position, at one speed, in one voice, at one volume, you're going to lose the audience. So don't do that!

## Come Back!

However, if you notice during your speech that you *have* lost your audience, don't despair. There's still time to bring them back and retrieve the success of the event.

Terri Brady says that a good way to tell when you've lost your audience is to listen for laughs after your jokes. If everyone laughs, they're probably still with you, and their patience will have been renewed by the joke itself. If nobody laughs, either you made a dumb joke or they aren't with you. In either case, there is an almost sure way to get them back.

This is a powerful secret, and it really works. If you ever feel like you've lost or are losing your audience, simply stop talking. Take a long pause. When the speaker is quiet, the people in the crowd stop thinking whatever is on their minds and look directly at the speaker.

The next words out of your mouth will make or break your speech. So say something noteworthy. Say your main point, the most important thing you have to say, the thing you truly care about most in your speech topic.

A good pause will get the crowd's attention, and after you make your extremely important statement, you can then just explain it—simply and directly.

This is really powerful. A good, long pause is generally very effective. Don't be afraid to wait for several seconds, or even a minute. If you give them silence for long enough, they'll come back to you, simply because they're worried they missed a question, or as Terri Brady puts it, "They think the teacher just called on them when they weren't paying attention."

Silence brings a feeling of high drama.

You can also handle these situations by changing up the tone or posture of your speech in any of the ways we discussed before: slow down or speed up, speak more quietly or loudly, or change your voice or inflection.

Another great way to get the audience back is to change your topic of discussion for a minute. Telling a story to restart their imagination and person-to-person relating can be extremely effective.

In fact, if you really need to fix a speech, choose a long silence followed by the words, "I need to tell you a story...." Then tell them your best story and explain it to them.

When you have them back, you can continue with your message, but be careful to stay interesting and engaging to this particular crowd.

## Before You Show Up

You should also take the specific nature of your audience into consideration as you get your speech ready. Whatever you want to teach them, present it in such a way that they'll want to hear about it and then change their lives or at least take specific action.

You shouldn't prepare a talk for six-year-olds if it's intended for adults and vice versa.

Know (to the best of your ability) who you'll be talking to before you get there so you can prepare the speech to be a good fit for the audience you're dealing with. And of course, preparing the speaker as well as the speech will help you deal with any surprises along the way.

## Not to Put Too Fine a Point on It

Lee Iacocca said, "There is no substitute for accurate knowledge. Know yourself, know your business, know your men." This is the message of this chapter. When it comes to effective SPLASH speaking, there really is no substitute for knowing yourself, your cause, and your audience.

And of course, you have to give the speech in a manner that really supports and emphasizes each of these.

To be really successful at this, present yourself and your cause to the audience in a way that really helps them *care*. Think about how to do this as you plan your talk.

The point is this: While your speech can and should help you with an overall cause you truly care about, it's not about you. If you don't make it about your audience, you aren't making it a success.

On the bright side, as you learn *how* to make it about them and start to apply those how-tos, your public speaking ability will grow exponentially, and your power to impact the world and the people in it will make huge strides forward.

Get to know your audience, and get them interested in what matters most!

# 15

## *The audience is the barometer of the truth.*

—BARBRA STREISAND

This quotation can be misleading if it suggests that there are no absolute truths, that truth is relative, or that what you say is only true if certain people agree with you.

On the other hand, there is something to be considered in this statement, something that is absolutely critical to speakers who plan to speak in a moving way to a crowd they ultimately hope to help. And that is the fact that the audience is only going to come away from your speech with the things they *learned*, no matter what you actually *said*.

> *The audience is only going to come away from your speech with the things they* **learned,** *no matter what you actually* **said.**

Read that last sentence again. It is worth repeating. This is very important, and good speakers never forget the difference. SPLASH speakers focus on what the audience will learn and how they'll change and not so much on what is said.

## Traps and Pitfalls

How can a speaker do this? To begin with, you have to know some real truth. Have an actual principle, not just something you made up because you thought the audience would laugh. As we've discussed in past chapters, your foundation as a speaker is some great cause or battle that you've dedicated your life to supporting.

In turn, the foundation for each speech is some small part of this cause that you can teach, achieve, or accomplish in the time allotted for your talk. Specifically, always choose some truth you want to teach the audience that will help them change their lives, make them better people, and ultimately get everyone closer to the victory of your cause. It's that simple!

> *It's better to have a thousand people who support the* **real** *mission than a hundred thousand who just like the arbitrary benefits.*

A word of caution: It's important that you don't give in to the temptation to corrupt or change your true message so that more people will agree with you. It's a good thing to sacrifice the little preferences that don't actually matter to your goals or cause and to pick your battles wisely instead of fighting over insignificant details. But you should never compromise the cause itself just to get more popularity, approval, or support.

It's better to have a thousand people who support the *real* mission than a hundred thousand who just like the arbitrary benefits. Perhaps you've seen the T-shirt or an Internet comic that has a picture of Darth Vader with a pile of chocolate chip cookies and text that reads, "Come to the Dark Side....We have cookies!" Guess what? If they join the dark side, or the light side, or any side for the sake of cookies, they're not really on a side (except for maybe the cookies'). If you have to catch them with fluff to get them to support your cause, they're probably not really supporting it. If you spend too much time catering to these halfhearted supporters, you'll often lose some of your natural allies—the ones who would have really helped advance the cause because they truly care.

Of course, there is nothing wrong with offering refreshments or making your speech fun. But always make sure you tell them the real message in a way that the true leaders will hear (even if they don't yet realize that they are leaders).

### Do!

What you absolutely must do is figure out how to explain the truth to the audience in such a way that they'll actually get it. The truth is not defined or decided by the audience; it doesn't change from one crowd to another. What does change is the way you explain it, the examples you give, the stories you tell, and everything else about how you convey the truth to them.

This is not a tool to help you switch your allegiance every five minutes. Rather, it's designed to help you target your argument to the people you're actually trying to convince.

Speeches should be a transfer of truth from you to them. The audience is the barometer of the truth in that they should be the way you gauge and plan the words you use to cast light on the truth.

When you do this, you actually have more likelihood of teaching the truth you intended to teach. After all, like studying art, public speaking, and in fact any teaching, is really not about what you say; it's about what the people hear and what they do about it.

As you plan for this and expect your audience to be a sort of barometer, you'll be better able to match what you say to what you *want* them to learn, so you can match it to what they *actually* do learn.

This gives you tremendous power to help and influence others in the right direction, instead of whatever random direction might pop into their heads.

# 16

## *The best speakers are the best listeners.*

### —TERRI BRADY

The lesson that the best speakers are the best listeners is simple but can really benefit you, especially as a beginning speaker. When Terri Brady said this, she was explaining the power of quoting other great speeches and books. She shared her love of hearing talks sprinkled with quotations from her favorites. She revealed how she'd be sitting in the audience and would suddenly say to herself, "This guy is a good speaker! He's quoting all my favorite people."

Some people get annoyed by quotations in speeches. And of course, you have to be careful not to overdo it and leave your audience feeling like they'd have done as well to see some other person speak, since you had nothing innovative to add. But overall, we believe that quoting excellent sources in your talk adds to the flavor and depth of the presentation.

This technique can be especially helpful if you know your audience well and can quote from people they care about. For example, you'll probably have more success quoting Canadian heroes to Canadians than to Australians.

## Information Galore

You should never have a hard time finding content for your speeches. Information, principles, and ideas are everywhere! If you're following the other tips and advice given in this book, you've already made it a priority to be reading and listening to great information on a regular basis, which means you're filling your mind with excellent quotes. This is going to be a big help to you as you start out on your SPLASH speaking journey.

As you read and listen, watching carefully for important concepts and ideas to share with future audiences, you'll be preparing yourself to use quotations that will leave your audience members saying, "This speaker's great! He's quoting everybody who's awesome!" And it will be even better when they say, "What a great quote! I really need to apply that in my life."

In doing this, you not only use content that clearly has great power—it obviously impacted you enough that you thought it was good speech material—but you'll also be able to send people to where they can get more information to help them choose the important changes you're inspiring them to go home and make.

This is essential if you want their experience to go beyond a standing ovation. If you can send your audience somewhere to get more of what they need to really benefit from your speech, in a way that makes your speech better, you're in a great place! And that's just what the appropriate use of quotations can do.

But how do you make it all *really* sink in?

# 17

## *You haven't told them till you've shown them.*

—CHRIS BRADY

As Chris Brady says, "Speaking is not a performance." So while you're onstage, it's necessary to resist the urge to merely perform. You may feel pleased after your speech that you had the crowd laughing all night, but that doesn't mean you did your job.

Maybe you did, maybe not. The laughter is a good sign, but did you use it to truly help the audience make important life changes?

On the other hand, if they were sleeping all through your speech, there's a pretty good chance you didn't get your point across very well in that situation either.

It is absolutely vital to use illustrations *well*. This is what makes a speech memorable. The illustration can be a story, a question, something you hold up in your hand for all to see, a diagram or chart on a whiteboard or PowerPoint presentation, or anything else that immediately captures the audience's attention and helps them remember what you have told them.

> *Be entertaining while resisting the urge to be simply an entertainer.*

The purpose of the illustration is to help the audience experience the speech deeply and memorably. As Brady says, the point of the illustration is to be entertaining while resisting the urge to be simply an entertainer.

To do this, you have to find the right balance of being entertaining coupled with effectively passing on deep and valuable meaning. As we discussed earlier, you're not standing up on a whim. You have an important message; you stand for something that truly matters.

If the audience hasn't received that, no matter how fun your speech was, you haven't really succeeded. Like a quarterback, you have to throw the ball in such a way that the receivers actually catch it—over and over and over.

And the illustrations you choose for your speech can make all the difference. In fact, as Chris Brady puts it, "I would say that the number one error made by public speakers is not using illustrations at all, or using insufficient illustrations."

## What It's All About

Success in speaking, while it may vary in specific intent, means that you genuinely inspire your audience to take action and make authentic changes in their lives. And these actions and changes should help further the important cause you share in your message.

If you're speaking to an audience, it should be because you have something to say that matters so much that you are not only *comfortable* asking them for this change, but you're uncomfortable *not* asking for it.

This matters!

This is the crux of great public speaking.

This is how you avoid the pitfalls of mere entertainment: stand for something you care about so much that you couldn't possibly let it go unsaid or uncommunicated.

## Show; Don't Tell

Of course, as we've said, an audience that laughs but doesn't learn is just as bad as a sleeping one. Neither of these groups catches your vision or implements anything you meant to teach.

In other words, you have to be entertaining enough that people actually listen. But remember that deep and genuine passion for a worthy cause is often one of the most "entertaining" things out there. A speaker who is truly passionate about his or her message is always better than one who isn't.

Your job as a speaker is to know what you're passionate about, figure out what your audience is passionate about, and then show them, in no uncertain terms, the connection between the two. If you do this, you'll be an excellent public speaker.

> *Your job as a speaker is to know what you're passionate about, figure out what your audience is passionate about, and then show them, in no uncertain terms, the connection between the two.*

Choose the right story or stories, word pictures that will become part of the audience's memory. Or use an appropriate quote and expound on it. Or put up a picture or chart for them to think about. Again, the right illustration is more memorable than anything else a speaker does.

Sometimes you emphasize the audience's passion to show them why they should be passionate about yours as well, and other times, you show them why they should be passionate about yours *instead*. This last one happens less frequently, and is much more difficult, but it can be done. The trick is to really *show* them why they should care—to help them *feel* it.

Ultimately, public speaking is about feeling. What the members of the audience feel *is* the speech, for them.

The right story, quotation, or other illustration makes them feel something in a way that the feeling will last. So each time you prepare a speech, ask yourself how good the illustration is. Will it immediately capture their attention? Will it burn into their memories? If not, keep brainstorming until you find the right one.

> *The right illustration is more memorable than anything else a speaker does.*

An excellent example of the "Show; Don't Tell" principle is Martin Luther King Jr. He knew how to clue in his audience to his vision. Picture him saying "I have a dream" over and over and then sharing his vision of a better nation and world.

When you get your audience to feel and see your vision, you're getting them on your side—really making them feel like your partner in the cause. When your audience feels like your partner, you're in a good place because they feel a responsibility for the failure or success of the cause. Such feelings are naturally followed by action.

Of course most of the time, the majority of these people will be at least slightly less dedicated to the cause than you are. Sturgeon's Law (90 percent of people don't do much) does apply in these situations as in all others.

But you will get a few people who will really make a difference, and even the limited support of the others is better than nothing. Plus, you never know who's going to be one of that 10 percent that'll take your message and run with it.

When Martin Luther King Jr. gave his "I Have a Dream" speech, he exemplified this principle of "Show; Don't Tell," and because of this, many people joined his cause. What did he do that made this more than an ordinary speech given to ordinary people and ultimately having an ordinary, small impact? This secret is very important: he invited us to share his vision.

We suggest that you find a video of this speech and watch it. The lessons you can learn from watching other greats do what you hope to master are countless. So while you're at it, watch videos of other great speeches as well.

Here are some of the ways King made his speech unforgettable and highly influential for thousands of minds over the years.

## Make Them Coconspirators

He opened by stating his vision for the speech's impact: He told the audience that they were part of a demonstration that would go down in history. By telling them that the event itself would have a SPLASH, he had already made them *feel* like his coconspirators, cofounders, and partners just by being there.

This is the same way King Henry V engages his soldiers in Shakespeare's play about him. In both cases, the audience members were instantly on the speaker's side, and not just as followers. The speakers made them feel like *leaders* in a noble cause.

Then Martin Luther King Jr. made it very clear what the cause was. Getting your audience to feel like leaders in the cause is probably the best way to make a real difference in public speaking because it's the best way to ensure further action after the clapping ends. This is powerful. In fact, this really is the whole point of most public speaking: to help the listeners stand up and take leadership in an area where they really should be leaders anyway.

**Symbolism and Metaphor**

The next way Dr. King spoke to the hearts of the audience was through the effective use of symbolism and metaphor. By employing symbolic language, rather than just bluntly stating every point, you'll turn on the more imaginative parts of the listeners' brains and speak directly to their hearts. When you paint a picture instead of simply listing your points a-b-c-d, you're *showing* them what you mean. This allows them to come up with the conclusions on their own, which strengthens their feelings of responsibility and call to action. Of course, a-b-c-d can be a good illustration too, especially if your goal is to get them to do four specific things.

> *Use an illustration that is immediately catchy and also lastingly memorable.*

When your audience draws the same conclusions you did from a story, metaphorical statement, list, or any other effective illustration, they feel that it was their idea— because it was! This is how leadership begins.

When your audience cares deeply about the cause because it was authentically their idea, sparked by something you shared, they're more likely to do something about it. Period.

Using stories, symbolism, metaphors, lists, quotes, personal experiences, and other creative illustrations is probably the best way to *show* them what you mean in unforgettable and undeniable ways.

## Relatable Specifics

The way King finished his speech was truly brilliant. By using widely known biblical references and referring to a well-known and beloved song, he related to the audience with illustrations they were already affectionately familiar with. But he took it a step further.

Although it gave him huge points and really caused a stir in his audience, it was not enough for him to simply say, "From every mountaintop, let freedom ring!" He went on to list, by name, several mountaintops across the United States. By mentioning mountains and hills in various states, he managed to speak to numerous hearts individually. Any member of his audience who had seen or lived near Stone Mountain of Georgia, Lookout Mountain of Tennessee, or any of the other specific mountains he named felt spoken to and recognized as an *individual*, not just as part of a crowd.

Great speakers combine a level of general and individual relatability. To do this, refer to people, places, or things everyone in your audience can instantly relate to, but also take some time to use more specific, individual references.

If you're speaking in Phoenix, for example, mention Scottsdale, Tempe, and Prescott. When you do this, even people from Chandler or Mesa will feel like you're talking directly to them.

In Atlanta, mention Forest Park and Athens, and even listeners from Gainesville or East Point will feel understood. In Ottawa, bring up Cumberland or Chelsea and know what you're talking about when you do this. Or maybe just mention the Suns, Falcons, or Senators.

Combining general and specific illustrations and examples will make a huge difference in your connection with the audience and your influence with them. Remember, you're talking to a crowd, but if you don't speak to individual members of that crowd, your impact will be diminished.

To accomplish this effectively, you have to know who your audience is—what kinds of illustrations will be meaningful to them as a whole and as individuals. But guess what? That's public speaking. You have to know your audience to be effective.

## Humor and Tears

In summary, SPLASH speakers have to balance audience interest and involvement with actual impact and depth. Some of your illustrations, references, and symbols will be jokes and funny stories. That's okay, and humor will make your speech better than if the whole thing were dry, boring, or too serious.

Have fun with the audience because laughter opens the mind and heart. Just remember that while they're laughing, they should also be *changing*.

To repeat: It's a great idea to tell jokes and funny stories that will make the audience like you and enjoy hearing what you say, but the humor shouldn't distract from your overall message and goal.

One of the best ways to help your audience relate to what you're saying is to tell them a funny story that seems to be there purely as entertainment, but then you weave it into the speech in such a way that it teaches an important lesson.

But *do* tie it in. Make it an integral part of your overall message. Audiences feel edified even more when they are able to enjoy a funny story that turns into a deep lesson in a surprising way that feels like some unintended twist.

By making the lessons fun, you're making them memorable. Just be sure the memories you're leaving are the ones that most benefit your cause, whatever it may be.

Another option is to occasionally use a key word or an acronym like SPLASH or E-I-E-I-O. This can be overdone, so only use it once in a while when it really seems to fit. Used correctly, this can be very memorable.

Again, the goal is to use an illustration that is immediately catchy and also lastingly memorable. Make sure every speech has such a central illustration.

Speakers are not entertainers. They're warriors for a cause. But frequently, the best way to win your battles is to gather an army of people who really care about your victory. The best, most effective way to do this is to make your speech interesting, catchy, important, real, entertaining, relatable, memorable, and *theirs*.

If you make your cause their cause, everybody wins.

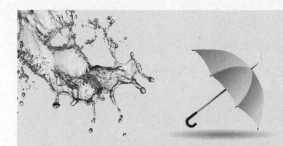

# SPLASH Zone!

1. Know what you stand for.

2. Take a real stand for your cause, and learn to promote it through public speaking.

3. Don't waste time on distractions.

4. Get your information, media, and examples from the right people and places.

5. Listen to feedback from the right people and improve your speaking as you learn from them. Be happy when the bad guys are your critics; this means you're making a real difference.

6. Prepare the speaker (you) for every speech by knowing how you want the audience to be changed when you finish speaking.

7. Before every speech, visualize how the audience will respond and what they'll do after they go home, and change your speech as needed to obtain this goal.

8. Learn something new and interesting about the topic before every speech.

9. If you are a beginning speaker, try writing out your talk in detail, then making an outline, and then throwing it all away before you go onstage. This process will help you prepare the speaker and not just the speech!

10. Make a point of dealing with the little, practical considerations that could distract your audience from your message.

11. Be centered on who you are and what you have to offer before you ever walk onstage. Remember that speaking is a privilege, a responsibility, and an honor, so focus on your purpose there, not your insecurities.

12. Be open to new thoughts and ideas that come to you as you're speaking; these are often the best segments of your talk.

13. Leave negatives and challenges backstage by creating a clear, strong vision and following it. Replace worries or concerns with a renewed focus on your speech's purpose.

14. If the audience isn't learning, you aren't teaching.

15. Use a good mixture of loud and soft, fast and slow, funny and serious, and talking and not talking to create a full, interesting, and complete experience.

16. Use humor, quotations, stories, metaphors, and symbols as needed to help the audience catch and share your vision.

# Simplicity Is Power

*There is no greatness where there is not simplicity,*
*goodness, and truth.*
—Leo Tolstoy

# 18

## *Naked lions are just as dangerous as elegantly dressed ones.*

—SUSAN CAIN

In all this use of metaphors and stories, along with listening to the new ideas that pop into your head onstage, it's easy to get caught in the traps of over-complication, showiness, and long-windedness. We advise that you do not let this happen. In the case of public speaking, as with so many other things, simplicity really is power.

As we learn from Occam's Razor, the simplest answer may not always be the correct one, but it generally leads to better understanding of the question and ultimately brings us to the right answer.

In speaking, one of your most important goals is communication with the audience, so clearly, the answer that brings the best understanding is an excellent place to start. This requires simplicity.

### Avoid Flashy

If you want to be an effective speaker, remember that it's *SPLASH* you want, not *flash*. You aren't trying to impress your audience with your intelligence, your fancy words, or your ability to speak for eight hours beyond your allotted time. One of the main enemies of simplicity is trying to sound smart, funny, or cool. In fact, getting right to the point is usually the best tip for great public speaking.

Your goal is to help them gain some new understanding, information, or commitment to your topic and to inspire them to make important changes in their lives. Nothing works better than honest, sincere, passionate simplicity.

In his book *The Articulate Executive*, Granville N. Toogood notes that top speakers have a special formula, a secret that most other speakers don't understand. Not knowing this secret keeps a lot of managers from ever becoming executives and a lot of mediocre public speakers from ever becoming great.

> *Nothing works better than honest, sincere, passionate simplicity.*

This secret enables anyone who knows it to immediately walk to the front and command a room, so that every attendee is instantly interested and hanging on every word. It helps a speaker influence any crowd so that those who heard even just one speech are behaving differently many years later—all because of what happened that day.

Those who don't know this secret will never be truly great speakers, while those who know and use it can't help but make a huge difference whenever they speak.

People who don't know this secret frequently just say that a certain speaker has "charisma," but in reality, charisma pretty much always comes from following the special formula.

Would anyone like to know what it is? Here's the secret: As Toogood said, great speakers "*add value* to what they are saying by *taking a position. They have a point of view. They translate situations into positions. They present evidence* to back up their position, then propose *a course of action. They speak simply.* They answer our objections before we can raise them. *They press the case with conviction. They believe.*"

In short, the secret is to boldly stand for something worthwhile—and to do it in such a way that people can relate.

Toogood continued:

And even if you feel you have no charisma—even if you hate to speak…—you can still far surpass your expectations and come across as a leader yourself.

> "*If you have something to say and say it well, the world will listen.*"
> —*Granville N. Toogood*

Some people believe that if Winston Churchill had not taken to the airwaves in WWII, Londoners would be speaking German today.…Billy Graham took his crusade to the world and…his ministry has forever changed the lives of millions of people.

If you have something to say and say it well, the world will listen.

This secret is a formula for SPLASH speaking:

- Add value by taking an important and strong position.
- Provide evidence for the position.

- Propose a good course of action.
- Speak simply and directly, and truly relate to the audience.
- Make your point with conviction.
- Say what you really believe.

This secret is actually kind of obvious when you think about it. But too often, we forget that honestly caring about something that really matters and then sharing it the best we can, over and over, is the key to success—not just great public speaking.

The rest is really just commentary on how to put this secret formula into action.

## The Two Audiences

But note that the reason this secret works is because each person in the audience is really two people: the conscious mind that listens and thinks and takes notes and the emotional mind below the surface that feels the primal pull of happiness, anger, frustration, sadness, peace, rejection, fear, joy, and enthusiasm.

And guess which of these two people you are really speaking to? The answer is, surprisingly, *both*. If you appeal to only one, whichever it is, you won't create a true SPLASH. It won't stick, or even if it does, it won't last. The ripples only spread when you hit both the conscious and the emotional person in every member of the audience.

When you take a stand for something important, share your passion and conviction, propose a good course of action, and convey your deep belief in how vital your words are, you are speaking to the emotional mind in each listener.

So when and how does a SPLASH speaker reach the conscious mind of the audience? This happens before the speech, or in a split second at the beginning of an impromptu speech, when the speaker asks, "Which kind of speech is this: know, feel, or do?"

## Know. Feel. Do.

It really is this simple. Which of these is the goal of your speech? Do you want the audience members to *know* something new when you're done? Or do you want them to *feel* something they'll never forget? And when you finish speaking and they return to their everyday lives, what do you want them to *do* differently?

All SPLASH speeches are "do" speeches, meaning that the listeners are changed by the speech, so they *do* something differently in their lives.

There are three distinct ways to get them to do things differently. With the first method, they'll change what they do because they know something now that they didn't know before. For example, when a man realizes there are personality types and that he is a certain type, while his spouse, coworkers, and children are different types, this information can help him greatly improve his relationships. The knowledge is powerful if he applies it.

A second path to engendering real change is to make them feel something so deeply that they never again want to settle for mediocrity. For example, when a person hears the story of how Thomas Jefferson's wife and daughter both died because he wrote the Declaration of Independence, it brings a feeling of reverence for freedom that most people don't have until they realize the price people have always had to pay to stay free.

The third way to change an audience with a speech is to combine both "know" and "feel" goals in the same talk. This is more difficult, so beginning speakers should focus on giving either "know and do" speeches or "feel and do" speeches.

## Putting It into Action: The Two Levels of Public Speaking

When you prepare your speech, immediately ask what you want the listeners to do after the speech is over. Then ask yourself which is the best way to help them make this change. Will they be more likely to take action if they learn something new or if they feel something very strongly?

When you know the answer to these questions, you can prepare your speech accordingly.

Then, after your speech, follow up and find out if it worked. Did the audience members apply what you wanted them to? Are they changed? If not, adjust your speeches until you get the results you really want.

This is the first level of public speaking. Give both kinds of speeches ("know and do" and "feel and do") until you become effective at helping audience members really change. Keep track, and work on improving the results.

The second level is similar: After you have given a number of successful speeches of both kinds (and you've followed up and know that the listeners are applying your messages), try preparing a speech that accomplishes all three goals in one talk: "know, feel, and do." Practice this until you become really good at it. This is SPLASH speaking.

As you are doing this, always keep in mind that it's essential to be easily relatable. Let's discuss a few ideas on how to do this most effectively.

## Be the Right Kind of Dumb

While it's naturally true that listeners who think a speaker is ignorant probably aren't going to be influenced by that person, it is also true that really intelligent speakers who focus too much on *sounding* smart aren't going to be very successful either. In fact, they won't seem nearly as intelligent as the speakers who focus on more important things, like their message and sharing it well with the audience.

As we learned earlier from Chris Brady, it's much better to *show* people than to tell them. This is especially true when it comes to your own smartness or intelligence.

When speakers have to tell the audience how smart they are, either in direct language or by trying to make intellectualizing, over-witty, über-educated, or showy remarks, the audience tends to believe they aren't very smart at all. Instead, demonstrate your intellect by delivering your important message simply, passionately, and with conviction.

### Humor *Them*, Not You

Again, while making the crowd laugh now and then can be a significant part of an effective speech, don't let yourself become nothing but an unskilled stand-up comedian. That's not what you're there for, and it doesn't help you.

Jokes or funny stories will often factor into your talks, but they should be natural and well-placed. Don't get into a habit of just indulging yourself with all your favorite jokes or looking for extra personal attention.

Often, beginning speakers try to start their speeches with jokes that really aren't very good. This is a bad idea for many reasons.

For one, when an opening joke falls flat, you as a speaker are often thrown off for a while because you didn't get the expected reaction. When this happens, you can waste time just trying to regain your footing—time you should be spending making meaningful connections with your audience.

Also, a bad joke throws the audience off as well. Listeners start thinking about their schedule for the day, their babysitter, or the reading materials on their lap. This isn't your best situation as a speaker.

A bad joke at the beginning also changes the audience from listeners to critics. They start analyzing you as a speaker instead of learning from your message.

## What Bingley Learned the Hard Way

There's a really funny scene in the 2005 production of *Pride and Prejudice* where Mr. Bingley comes to propose to Jane, but things don't go quite as he had pictured them.

He enters the Bennets' living room and offers his greetings. Unfortunately, Mrs. Bennet doesn't say what he expected her to say, so he ends up excusing himself very awkwardly and heading home after just a few minutes, without proposing.

He then proceeds to take what seems like half an hour or more getting past the fact that Jane's mother didn't say, "Sit down," and trying to plan and role-play his next visit so that everything will work nicely.

He tries to use a gimmicky sort of plan that specifically depends on others acting in a certain way, and when things don't work out as he envisioned, he not only fails in his plan of action but has to go away and restructure his entire strategy.

This is a luxury you won't usually have if the audience doesn't respond to the first five minutes of your speech the way you wanted them to.

Interestingly, when Bingley eventually comes back, he employs a much simpler and therefore much better and more effective strategy.

He walks in and simply requests an audience with the girl he hopes to marry. He says exactly what he wants and what he means in such a way that nobody can accidentally ruin it by misunderstanding him or thinking he is being sneaky or weird.

Simplicity is power when what you say is truly important. What is especially telling about Bingley's second approach is the result: he finds himself engaged to Jane within minutes.

Simplicity works!

## Distractions Tend to Distract

Likewise, don't try to distract your audience from your point by making weird jokes or comments because you'll probably succeed.

If a story, comment, or joke naturally supports your real message and point, it's okay to use it—as long as you don't use too many. But if you're using it just for effect, it will usually distract both you and your audience from what really matters. For example, a young man who was asked to give a speech stood up and told the audience: "Please stand. Now take a step to the left. Now step to the right. Okay, sit down." After everyone was reseated, he said, "Now you can never say that my speech didn't move you."

A few people giggled, but many of the audience members looked at each other awkwardly. Then the speaker went on to give a good, very enjoyable speech.

But the only thing most people remembered was the awkward beginning.

In contrast, a different person who was speaking at the end of a lengthy seminar stood, smiled at the audience, and said, "We've been sitting here for a long time this afternoon. Why doesn't everyone stand for a few seconds and rest your personality?"

Everyone laughed at this unique turn of phrase, and the whole audience was grateful for the chance to stretch their legs. While having the crowd focus on something that's not part of the speech is seldom a good idea, in this situation, it really hit the spot.

When the speaker saw that everyone was ready to begin, he asked them to sit. Then he said, "Today, I'm going to change your life." Then he stopped for a long pause.

The crowd was hooked. Almost everyone unconsciously leaned forward in their chairs and watched his face with rapt attention.

When he began speaking again, everyone listened.

If the speaker had then begun talking about something without passion, or if he had tried to use gimmicks to make his point, he would have lost the audience. Fortunately, he knew why he was there and what message he wanted to share, so he delivered a moving speech—a SPLASH speech.

## What *Does* Work

What most effectively replaces all the gimmicks, witty comments, and other distractions is real and genuine interest in your topic. If you try to impress your audience with flash, you probably won't impact them much.

So get up there, be natural, put all the extras aside, and speak from your heart about something that is truly important to you. This is the great secret of public speaking: say something that matters, simply and with passion, after preparing well beforehand.

When you do this, you will leave the only real impression that matters. And interestingly enough, most people will actually think you're smarter, funnier, and even *more* impressive than you actually are. The SPLASH will do the work for you.

As you focus on impact, on truly helping the audience, the impressiveness of your excellence will take care of itself, and you'll be the kind of SPLASH speaker the world really needs—the kind that's ready and able to make a real difference for good.

# 19

## *No one ever complains about a speech being too short!*

—IRA HAYES

Another common pitfall in public speaking, especially when you've embraced the important concept that ideas come from everywhere, is the tendency to say way too much. When you do this, you often lose your audience, dilute your message, and weaken your speech.

Obviously, these are outcomes you should probably avoid if you want to be a SPLASH speaker.

To begin with, most people have about an eight-second window and then an eighteen-minute window. This is why starting a speech with gimmicks can really backfire.

Audiences tend to sum up a speaker in the first eight seconds, so if your message is really important, just stand up and tell them so—first thing. By the way, this also makes you look more like a leader. Most of the best leaders got there by saying what really matters directly, simply, and repeatedly.

In addition to the eight-second window in which listeners decide how much to care about any speech, there is also an eighteen-minute window. Most people don't want to hear any one message for longer than this.

The key to great speaking is to break longer speeches into chunks of eighteen minutes or less, so people feel a shift of direction at least every eighteen minutes.

For example, the first eighteen minutes might empha-size the message, the next eighteen might present evidence and stories that support the message, and a final eighteen minutes might provide solutions.

But the best speakers take this a step further by reversing this order. They tell you in the first eight seconds what the problem is and in the first eighteen minutes what the solution is. The rest of the speech, which is made a lot shorter with this format, focuses on evidence, stories, and support for the solution.

## Which Ideas Matter

When you're speaking and you have a hundred new ideas floating around in your mind, it's important to sort out which ones to tuck away for future consideration and use and which ones to incorporate into your current speech.

While it's true that many thoughts that come to you can have important lessons and meaning for you and your audiences, it is not true that every one of them has relevance to the talk you're actually giving or to the audience you're serving at the moment. So even if every idea is a good one, you have to filter which ones are appropriate for *right now*.

The easy way to do this is to remember your predefined measure of success for this speech. What was the desired impact that directed your preparation before you got onstage? What do you want the listeners to do?

Whatever questions or filters you used to decide what to say while you were preparing can be applied to the last-minute inspiration that hits you during your speech. Is this a "know" speech or a "feel" speech or both? And again, what do you want the audience members to do? If the new idea that comes to you doesn't fit with your plan and bring them to that successful end, don't say it.

## Complicated Strays

Of course, there's another, more complicated part of this process. Every now and then, something will come to you as you are speaking that has no apparent connection to what you're trying to accomplish, but it keeps pestering you, and you really think you should say it.

If a thought persistently presents itself to you, begging to be said, there's a good chance that someone in your audience really needs it, regardless of its seeming randomness.

That's why it's important to be open to these ideas, and it's okay to go on strange tangents when you feel it's essential or necessary. Just make sure you don't spend more time on one than it really needs.

The crucial point of all this is that you don't give time to things that will unnecessarily distract from your end goal. Say no to thoughts that aren't a good addition to your current speech, and revisit them later for another talk (if at all).

Say yes to ideas and thoughts that are in keeping with your plan and message, and allow yourself to improvise important extras when it matters.

## When It's Time to Sit Down

It's generally a good idea to stop talking when your allotted time is up. You have a sort of unspoken—or sometimes spoken—agreement with your audience to free them from your speech after a certain amount of time, and you don't want to damage trust by breaking that commitment.

Plan your content in such a way that it can fit into your specified allotment, allowing some extra minutes for any spontaneous additions that may come up, and make a point of following this plan.

The instances when you should go over your time are extremely rare, so make a point of not doing so. This builds trust and positive energy between you and the audience.

Also, when you have said everything you have to say, don't be afraid to call it good, even if you have ten minutes left on the clock. You should never be onstage trying to merely fill time. Just conclude strongly and take a seat. That's good speaking!

You may have some important last thoughts that come up that you hadn't intended to say but find yourself wanting to share now that there's time. In that case, it's certainly okay to say them. That's why they gave you the time, to say what you have to say.

But don't try to fill extra time with nonsense or fluff. Sit down with a powerful ending and the important quality of every word you said having value. Don't ruin your SPLASH with a bunch of wimpy waves that leave no ripples.

It's better to say really great and important things for forty-five minutes and then sit down and let the audience leave with your vital message on their minds than to give the same excellent forty-five minutes followed by fifteen minutes of blahblahblah.

If this feels offensive to you right now reading this, imagine how the audience feels!

In short, plan your message to fit in the time you have been given to present it, and sit down when you're finished delivering your content, even if there's still time left because, as Ira Hayes put it, "No one ever complains about a speech being too short!"

# 20

## *Why doesn't the fellow who says "I'm no speechmaker" let it go at that instead of giving a demonstration?*
### —KIN HUBBARD

Another minor but practical detail that can make you a much better speaker is paying attention to how you present your authority to the audience. As we've just discussed, it's not a good idea to get up and tell them how smart you are and how edified they will be from spending a few minutes in your glorious presence. It's much better to share your important message and let them naturally discover what you have to offer.

On the other hand, however, if you stand up and tell them they're stupid if they listen to a word you say, they probably won't listen; in fact, they probably *shouldn't*.

### Disclaimers Are Disclaimers

Starting your speech with a disclaimer about your lack of preparation, lack of knowledge on the topic, or lack of worthiness to present is generally a bad plan. Likewise, saying that you only agreed to give this talk because somebody made you doesn't inspire confidence. When you do these things, you instantly make the audience doubt whether they should listen to what you have to say.

While self-deprecating humor can be a good way to teach certain principles and get the audience to relate to you, "self-discreditation" is almost never a good idea.

If you plan to give a speech on something evil and hope nobody will trust you, you might want to point out your many flaws right up front. Or better still, just don't give the talk. Bad practice makes you a bad speaker.

On the other hand, if you have an important message to share, one that matters to you and the future, don't ruin your chances of spreading its truth by telling everyone to run in terror from your speech.

## Do Something about It!

If you aren't prepared to speak, you should go get prepared before you walk onstage! Even if you don't, you still ought to be able to say something from your heart that's more valuable than "You should all go home and watch TV instead of listening to me because I'm a complete idiot" or any variation on this theme.

We're spending a lot of time on this because an amazing number of speeches start out with the speaker outlining reasons why the talk might not be very good. Try not to spread this disease, if at all possible.

If you feel you don't know enough about the topic, go learn more before you take the spotlight. If you are nervous, that's okay. But telling the audience how nervous you are doesn't help anyone. Just launch into your important message, and as you really get into it, your nervousness won't matter.

Finally, if you feel unqualified for the honor of the speaking engagement, you should do something about it! If you are genuinely unqualified to speak in front of the crowd, you need to get qualified before you show up, or just decline the offer outright.

In this way, "Simplicity Is Power" has to meet up with all the previous aspects of SPLASH speaking, most particularly "Leave It All Backstage."

When you stand up to speak, the time for complaining or worrying about your speaking shortcomings is long past. Now is the time to bring what you have and do your absolute best to serve and move the audience in all the right ways.

### Clarified Quality

It's imperative to note that "qualified" doesn't have to mean perfect. Being qualified doesn't mean you have to know everything there is to know about a topic or that you are the best public speaker in the world.

It means having an important and well-thought-out message that the audience really needs to hear and the willingness to put yourself out there to help them.

# 21

## *Don't whip with a switch that has the leaves on, if you want it to tingle.*

—HENRY WARD BEECHER

L et's spend just a minute discussing other flashy de-
vices speakers use that often end up seeming like
gimmicks or tricks and distracting or even detract-
ing from the real message.

One of the biggest of these is visual aids.

### Good or Bad?

Visual aids can be good when they are used specifically
to keep the speaker and the audience on track. Sometimes
using a PowerPoint presentation that includes quotations and pictures will really help you, as the speaker, to
remember all the important details you need to include in
your talk.

It can also keep the audience with you, especially when
you have people who do better with visual rather than
just auditory input or when your presentation is highly
technical.

On the other hand, these add-ons are often just a distraction. They can take a lot of time that would be better spent
simply speaking, and they can also tend to keep you from
effectively making your point.

If you find that you end up rambling through your entire speech when you don't have anything to keep you on track, it's probably a good idea to look into some solutions that will help you make your point more effectively and, especially, more concisely. This may need to be visual aids, either for your sake or the audience's, but sometimes a well-learned outline (as discussed in previous chapters) will do as well. Just learn what works for you, and make sure you plan accordingly.

The rule on visual aids is that using things like PowerPoint slides makes you seem more like an expert, while just speaking directly and simply about pivotal solutions makes you look like a leader.

This is an important distinction because very few people really want to follow an expert. They like their leaders to have proven expertise, but they want to really listen to and learn from leaders much more than from experts.

To combine these, don't take planned visual aids, but use a white board or overhead projector and just put up a few notes or diagrams in your own handwriting. Most leaders do this at times, but few make it to top leadership posts by planning out extensive graphics or slides.

Leaders know their speaking time is valuable, and they focus on just saying what they have to say, not trying to wrap it up in pretty or high-tech bows. If this seems counterintuitive to what you learned in a public speaking class, remember that top leaders do it this way.

## The Golden Rule of Simplicity

Whether for stories, jokes, comments, self-deprecations, visual aids, or anything else, follow this rule:

*Give the absolute simplest presentation that can effectively express, communicate, and translate your important point to the hearts and minds of your audience.*

If you can do this without visual aids, jokes, or other extras, you should. In fact, if you can do it without a speech—perhaps with a five-minute conversation with the two people in the audience who actually care—you should even do that and give your speech on some other subject.

Besides, the best jokes are nearly always those that arise naturally as you speak, not the ones you planned to tell.

The idea is not to give the most fantastic and epic performance imaginable; it is to make an impact that causes a real SPLASH. Everything in public speaking is about that.

If you, your audience, or your message requires visual aids to be effective, use them! The same is true for any other tool, technique, or tip anyone ever uses in public speaking or any kind of communication.

> *The best jokes are nearly always those that arise naturally as you speak, not the ones you planned to tell.*

Of course, you shouldn't hurt or limit your speech by excluding the things that will make it succeed. But if you're not saying things in the simplest and most inspiring way that does them justice, you're not saying them as well as you could, and you're probably wasting a lot of time and energy in the process.

## E-I-E-I-O

Chris Brady teaches the following guidelines to help you make sure you cover all the vital points and angles in your speech and then sit down when you are done. The key is to remember Old MacDonald's farm:

**E: Educate.** Make sure you give them something they didn't have before.

**I: Illustrate.** If it isn't illustrated with a story (or some other device), it will not be remembered.

**E: Entertain.** If you don't hold their attention (by making it fun, etc.), they won't pay attention to the content.

**I: Inspire.** Passion always has a part to play in transferring a message.

**O: Outcome.** What specific action are you calling the audience to take as a result of your talk?

If you've hit each of these steps in a simple but hard-hitting and straightforward way, you're probably pretty close to a good and effective speech.

Obviously, you may have more to learn and more practice hours to put in before you're a master, but making sure to check off each of these guidelines for each speech, and not trying to overdo it by adding much more, is the right kind of practice to eventually get you to that mastery level.

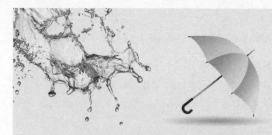

# SPLASH Zone!

1. Know what you stand for.

2. Take a real stand for your cause, and learn to promote it through public speaking.

3. Don't waste time on distractions.

4. Get your information, media, and examples from the right people and places.

5. Listen to feedback from the right people and improve your speaking as you learn from them. Be happy when the bad guys are your critics; this means you're making a real difference.

6. Prepare the speaker (you) for every speech by knowing how you want the audience to be changed when you finish speaking.

7. Before every speech, visualize how the audience will respond and what they'll do after they go home, and change your speech as needed to obtain this goal.

8. Learn something new and interesting about the topic before every speech.

9. If you are a beginning speaker, try writing out your talk in detail, then making an outline, and then throwing it all away before you go onstage. This process will help you prepare the speaker and not just the speech!

10. Make a point of dealing with the little, practical considerations that could distract your audience from your message.

11. Be centered on who you are and what you have to offer before you ever walk onstage. Remember that speaking is a privilege, a responsibility, and an honor, so focus on your purpose there, not your insecurities.

12. Be open to new thoughts and ideas that come to you as you're speaking; these are often the best segments of your talk.

13. Leave negatives and challenges backstage by creating a clear, strong vision and following it. Replace worries or concerns with a renewed focus on your speech's purpose.

14. If the audience isn't learning, you aren't teaching.

15. Use a good mixture of loud and soft, fast and slow, funny and serious, and talking and not talking to create a full, interesting, and complete experience.

16. Use humor, quotations, stories, metaphors, and symbols as needed to help the audience catch and share your vision.

17. Good public speaking is about SPLASH, not flash. Don't focus on impressing the audience; focus on moving them.

18. Don't spend extra time on ideas or concepts that don't help your message along. It's okay to save some ideas for later.

19. Make a point of keeping your speech within the time allotted, and don't be afraid to sit down whenever your message has been delivered; no one ever complains about a speech being too short!

20. Don't brag or make disclaimers about yourself or your lack of preparation to the audience. Let your content and performance speak for themselves.

21. Deliver your message in the simplest and most inspiring way that effectively transfers it to your audience. Don't use jokes, visual aids, stories, comments, or ideas that unnecessarily complicate your point. Remember to E-I-E-I-O!

# Happen!

*Apparently there is nothing that cannot happen today.*
—Mark Twain

# 22

## *Do one thing every day that scares you.*

—ELEANOR ROOSEVELT

The word *Happen*! in the SPLASH acronym actually serves three purposes because there are three ways that you have to really "Happen" if you want to make a lasting SPLASH in any speech.

### 1. Make It an Event!

First of all, to be an effective public speaker, you have to leave the audience feeling that your speech was a real event in their lives. They have to go home and think about it and tell their spouses, children, friends, and coworkers. They have to remember your speech and say, "Wow! That happened!" or "Hey, honey, remember that speech by…? That was so great! I haven't been the same since I heard it."

"Oh, you're right. That's when I first decided to really…"

And so on.

If the speech isn't a bold headline in their minds, you probably didn't Happen as fully as you must to make a true SPLASH. If a tree falls in the forest and nobody hears it, it probably doesn't matter much if it happened.

Your speech should be one that Happens, meaning that those who hear it know it—and never forget it! Great speeches are big events in our lives. That's the first kind of Happen!

## 2. Dive In!

The second type of Happen that's vital to every effective speech is pretty simple: You have to make sure your speeches actually do happen. If you never get up and speak in front of an audience, you'll never be a SPLASH speaker. Period.

To make your speeches Happen in this way, you have to be preparing yourself in all the other areas covered in this book, but you also have to be actively seeking opportunities to get in front of a crowd and actually speak.

You have to just do it. Even if you're bad at it. Even if you need lots of improvement. *Especially if you need lots of improvement.* Your speeches have to happen! You have to speak, and as often as you can. Be sure to stand for something that matters and to practice the other keys to great speaking, but don't just think about these things. Get in front of an audience, even a small one, and speak.

In fact, learn to speak well with smaller audiences, as many as you can. Make it happen!

Let's go back to where we started for a moment, with the discussion of stage fright and the funny quote from Jerry Seinfeld about preferring death to public speaking. We know you might be scared to get into the world of public speaking, but if you want to become an effective speaker and leader, there's an almost certain chance that you need to Happen as a speaker. So do it! Whatever the obstacles, get out and speak. And often!

As we already said, you'll probably start in smaller groups at first and then work your way up to bigger ones. That's great! It'll give you the practice to hone both your skills and your message so you'll be ready for the biggest SPLASHes of your life when the time is right!

### 3: Make It a Mastermind!

The third way that great speakers Happen is that they learn as they speak. They've done so much preparation, they care so much about the message and the members of the audience, and they feel so much energy from their own passion and the response of the crowd that they sometimes have epiphanies as they are speaking.

In such situations, speakers gain real, often cutting-edge insight into important ideas about the topic, the people, and the great cause they support.

If you've ever witnessed a speaker having such an experience, you know it feels magical for everyone in the room. A new level of excitement, depth, and wisdom seems to take over the whole meeting.

As a speaker, you can't really plan this, or it usually won't come. But when you truly prepare, deeply care about the topic and the listeners, and have paid a real price in your life to take a stand for something that really matters, this level of Happen can occur quite often.

Some top speakers and leaders measure every speech by this ruler: Is it truly life-changing for nearly everyone in the room? When this occurs, something genuinely incredible has happened.

Above all, when the speaker is changed by the talk—to the point that he or takes action afterward to make it last—this is a truly great speech.

There is an old saying that the teacher always learns more than the student. But there is actually a deeper reality here.

> *Some top speakers and leaders measure every speech by this ruler: Is it truly life-changing for nearly everyone in the room?*

Such change—where the speaker and all the audience members are never again the same—happens more often in smaller meetings where everyone in attendance has had to earn the right to be there and is in some way performing at a very high level. Somehow the effort and excellence of everyone combines so the speaker delivers an inspiring and life-changing message and at the same time learns even more than the audience—and then shares this new wisdom with everyone. This is a powerful experience that can only be described as magical, charismatic, or downright amazing.

Not surprisingly, this almost never happens unless the speaker and most of the people listening are applying the basics, doing the little things that always bring real success.

# 23

## *I never made one of my discoveries through the process of rational thinking.*

—ALBERT EINSTEIN

O rrin Woodward says, "If you want to get good at anything, you better get going!" Well, if you want to get good at public speaking, you better get started because as long as you're not going anywhere, you probably won't get very far.

Albert Einstein taught that the big discoveries aren't made simply by someone *thinking* about them; you have to start *doing* something. Another lesson we could learn from Einstein's life and experiences is that failure is just another step in the right direction.

Everyone can relate to this. As you take the steps toward becoming a SPLASH speaker, you're going to give a few SPLAT speeches, a few FLASH speeches, and probably some speeches you'll just plain want to forget. Fantastic! These are giving you the experience you need to make your talks Happen better than ever!

Unless you move beyond thinking about what speeches you'll someday give and start giving some now, your speaking career will be a rather uneventful one. If you are already giving speeches, start applying the various methods listed in this book. Doing so will have a huge and immediate impact on your speaking.

But some SPLAT speeches will occur, so as you encounter failing speeches, learn from them! And then move on. Keep trying. Rational thinking shouldn't be used as a reason to avoid public speaking or as an excuse to never forget old disappointments.

## Get Everyone Wet

Public speaking can be incredibly fun and exciting, and as you learn and apply the principles of SPLASH speaking, these instances will increase. But more important, public speaking also has the power to make a difference in the lives of countless individuals—especially your own life, whether you're the speaker or part of the audience.

> *Public speaking has the power to make a difference in the lives of countless individuals.*

Whichever you are, make sure you embrace the power of learning and self-improvement that comes from SPLASH speaking. Take responsibility for being the person who is entirely soaked when the speech is over, whether you delivered it or listened to it.

SPLASH speaking changes lives!

# 24

## *Things do not happen.*
## *Things are made to happen.*
### —John F. Kennedy

If you want to be great at this, to be a true *master*, you're going to have to make a lot of little things Happen, which will eventually lead to bigger, more substantial things.

To become a master speaker, as in anything else, you have to put in some focused hours preparing for and giving speeches. If you want to master the kind of speaking that creates a SPLASH, you have to get started.

> *In order to be a truly great public speaker, you have to speak publically—in front of an audience—at least once a week.*

Bestselling author and successful business leader Grant Cardone teaches that in order to be a truly great public speaker, you have to speak publically—in front of an audience—at least once a week.

Sometimes these speeches might be short, while others will probably be longer, but by developing a habit of weekly performance and practice, you'll be cultivating a good, solid ability to create quite a SPLASH!

If this means just sharing something important with a friend or family member at least once a week, do it. Look for opportunities to happen, and then go Happen!

## The Strong Finish

One of the most effective ways to make your speech Happen is to deliver a strong, memorable finish. In *The Articulate Executive*, Granville N. Toogood says there are six ways to do this well:

1. "Summarize your key point or key points." It is important to keep this short, but you can really emphasize your main points if you review each of them with passion.

2. "Loop back to the beginning." If you started with a story or statistic, or even a diagram or quote, consider recalling it at the end. Again, do this with emphasis to make it memorable.

3. "Ask the audience to do something." This is our favorite because it leaves them with the clear choice to act.

4. "Appeal to the positive." If the message of your speech was bad news, try to end by looking on the bright side and leaving them with something positive to do that can help the situation.

5. "Project." Focus on the future, and tell your listeners what they can do to bring about a better future.

6. "Tell a story that embraces your theme." This can be a very powerful tool, but it is essential to pick the right story and tell it the right way.

A good conclusion leaves the listeners excited and committed to take action, to change, to do things that will make a real difference. This is key to making things Happen as a speaker. Make your conclusion strong, and people will frequently act on it.

Think of the best speeches you've ever heard, and they almost certainly had strong, moving conclusions.

Now think about and apply the various principles of SPLASH speaking covered in this book. Get out your pen and highlighter and mark up quotations, methods, ideas, sentences, and sections that resonate with you. Then apply them.

Make public speaking happen in your life. Make it Happen! Otherwise, it won't.

# 25

## *The unexamined life is not worth living.*

—SOCRATES

In all this Happening, it's important that you also take the opportunity to improve your future speeches. The book *Mentoring Matters* provides excellent advice on how good public speakers can use the time right after they sit down from their speech to really hone their skills for future improvement:

Dale Carnegie said, "There are always three speeches for every one you actually gave. The one you practiced, the one you gave, and the one you wish you gave." Almost everyone who ever gives a speech, whether good or bad, sits down to the ovation of the audience and outwardly braves the storm of inner commentary. As he walks to his chair, he bombards himself with a list of things he should have said better or differently or not at all.

A good mentor teaches her mentee to smile at the commentary and take notes. This is one of the most powerful aspects of public speaking that a mentor can teach her mentee. How many times has he sat for hours with writer's block, trying to come up with the right words to express his message? And now, all of a sudden, he is hit with a seemingly never-ending burst of inspiration!

Mentors should teach their mentees to take full advantage of the after-speech siege of beautiful phrases and powerful expression. Some of the best stuff a speaker comes up with often comes in a fit of post-speech self-critique.

It's important that mentors help their mentees see this self-critique in a positive light. If a mentee feels like a complete loser after every speech because he is too critical of himself, it will likely be more hurtful than constructive. The moments after a speech should be seen as inspiration time, not self-destruction time....

Mentors should also try to set aside time to meet with their mentee after each speech and give him any other praise, critique, or commentary they feel will help the speaker's skills.

In critique and constructive criticism, it is important for mentors to be tactful and loving. The mentor should not attack the mentee with more than he can handle. Advice should be given in manageable chunks, determined by the mentee's own level of readiness. Mentors can be firm, but they should avoid being hurtful. This should be a time for building, not tearing down.

While this excerpt is from a book on mentoring and focuses on what mentors can do to help their mentees hone their skills after speaking, it can certainly be applied by individuals hoping to improve their own skills and success as speakers.

Using these techniques and guidelines to dissect and critique your own speeches after every talk is a great way to make today's Happening lift tomorrow's speeches to a whole new level of SPLASH.

All great leaders understand the necessity of getting feedback and becoming better after each speech. Those who fail to adjust and improve seldom succeed.

# 26

*They may forget what you said,
but they will never forget
how you made them feel.*

—CARL W. BUECHNER

L earning to help people feel deeply as you speak is vitally important to your success as a warrior-speaker.

With everything else you do, as you make a point of saying something that matters, preparing yourself to face all sorts of challenges as a speaker, speaking from your heart (not just your notes), remembering to serve and communicate with the audience, and doing these in the simplest and most effective way, don't forget that what you're really there to do is convey a feeling.

As many leaders have taught throughout history, people forget what you say or do, but they will remember how they felt and how you changed them forever.

Orrin Woodward said something along these same lines: "People will forget what you kept, but they will remember what you gave."

## If They Haven't Felt It, They Don't Care

To truly Happen as a speaker, you have to learn how to help people feel something. They may think things or learn things or even want things, and hopefully they do, but unless you can also inspire them to come away with the right feelings, they probably won't ever do much in reaction to your speech.

We've all heard that people buy emotionally, not logically. There are ways you can argue against that, and of course, everyone works differently, but the idea has merit. Perhaps the best way to express it is that people tend to buy emotionally and then defend their decisions logically.

It's important to make a logical case for points in your speeches because people need that too, and it will even help the emotional part along. But if you don't make your audience *feel* anything, you really haven't *done* anything because when it comes right down to it, if they don't *feel* anything, they still don't truly *care*.

## When People Care, Things Happen

If you want people to join a great cause, to change their lives, or to make the world a better place because they heard your speech, you have to help them care about the cause. And you do that by making them *feel* it.

So leave your audience with the flavor of the cause you stand for. Let them feel it in their hearts; make it matter to them. The extent to which you do this is the extent to which you Happen as a speaker.

And in many ways, the extent to which you Happen is the extent to which you SPLASH. Feeling is the biggest part of Happening, so go make it happen!

Watch their eyes while you speak, and learn to read their body language so you can just keep saying whatever is needed to get them to truly care. When you see this happen, when the whole audience Happens, leans forward, and turns passionate, you've made a SPLASH.

This isn't just a symbol or metaphor. It's very real, and good speakers learn to see it physically happen in an audience. Then they weave their speech and deliver it with this in mind—adjusting onstage until it happens.

> *Leave your audience with the flavor of the cause you stand for. Let them feel it in their hearts; make it matter to them.*

When you apply these principles and master the ability to do this, you can make every speech a SPLASH.

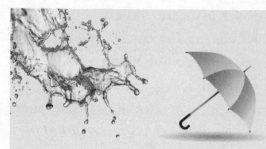

# SPLASH Zone!

1. Know what you stand for.

2. Take a real stand for your cause, and learn to promote it through public speaking.

3. Don't waste time on distractions.

4. Get your information, media, and examples from the right people and places.

5. Listen to feedback from the right people and improve your speaking as you learn from them. Be happy when the bad guys are your critics; this means you're making a real difference.

6. Prepare the speaker (you) for every speech by knowing how you want the audience to be changed when you finish speaking.

7. Before every speech, visualize how the audience will respond and what they'll do after they go home, and change your speech as needed to obtain this goal.

8. Learn something new and interesting about the topic before every speech.

9. If you are a beginning speaker, try writing out your talk in detail, then making an outline, and then throwing it all away before you go onstage. This process will help you prepare the speaker and not just the speech!

10. Make a point of dealing with the little, practical considerations that could distract your audience from your message.

11. Be centered on who you are and what you have to offer before you ever walk onstage. Remember that speaking is a privilege, a responsibility, and an honor, so focus on your purpose there, not your insecurities.

12. Be open to new thoughts and ideas that come to you as you're speaking; these are often the best segments of your talk.

13. Leave negatives and challenges backstage by creating a clear, strong vision and following it. Replace worries or concerns with a renewed focus on your speech's purpose.

14. If the audience isn't learning, you aren't teaching.

15. Use a good mixture of loud and soft, fast and slow, funny and serious, and talking and not talking to create a full, interesting, and complete experience.

16. Use humor, quotations, stories, metaphors, and symbols as needed to help the audience catch and share your vision.

17. Good public speaking is about SPLASH, not flash. Don't focus on impressing the audience; focus on moving them.

18. Don't spend extra time on ideas or concepts that don't help your message along. It's okay to save some ideas for later.

19. Make a point of keeping your speech within the time allotted, and don't be afraid to sit down whenever your message has been delivered; no one ever complains about a speech being too short!

20. Don't brag or make disclaimers about yourself or your lack of preparation to the audience. Let your content and performance speak for themselves.

21. Deliver your message in the simplest and most inspiring way that effectively transfers it to your audience. Don't use jokes, visual aids, stories, comments, or ideas that unnecessarily complicate your point. Remember to E-I-E-I-O!

22. Clarify beforehand whether the main point of your speech is to get people to know or feel and what exactly you want them to do. Then build your speech accordingly.

23. In order to change people through speaking, you have to actually get out and speak.

24. By actively searching for opportunities to speak in front of people, you'll gain valuable practice in public speaking.

25. A good way to improve your speaking is to take advantage of the moments right after you're done to take mental notes of what you can do better next time.

26. If you want people to do something about what you taught them, you have to make them really care; they have to truly feel it.

27. People change when something Happens to them, and the ultimate purpose of a speech is to create just such an event. When they are touched, taught, and transformed, when they go home and make real and lasting changes—this is when a speech is effective.

28. Be a SPLASH speaker:


**S**ay something that matters.

**P**repare the speaker, not just the speech.

**L**eave it all backstage.

**A**udience is everything.

**S**implicity is power.

**H**appen!

# EPILOGUE

At Sea World, the bleachers at the front of the stadium are marked "Splash Zone." This warns people who don't want to get wet to go sit somewhere up in the cheap seats.

But invariably, at almost every show, the seats in the Splash Zone are crammed full of excited people who can't wait to get wet! That's how life should be, in families and in education, career, and business, not just at theme parks.

Perhaps the most important thing we can tell you as you finish this book and head out to make thousands of little ripples is that the simple act of diving in makes an enormous SPLASH, and sitting in the SPLASH Zone is a sure way to get wet.

If you feel unsure of yourself, if you don't know whether you're ready to dive in, remember this: Soaked is soaked. If you're putting yourself in a position to be most influenced by true SPLASH speakers, you're sitting in the SPLASH Zone.

And once you're soaked (by their example), you may as well dive in and make a SPLASH of your own.

In fact, if you truly care about your future and your family and your cause and you really want to make a difference, you should consider the role of the whale trainers at Sea World. They spend their days helping others learn to make the most powerful SPLASHes—the ones that get rows of people drenched in their freezing water every day. By understanding the principles behind effective SPLASHing, the trainers are able to teach them to others, and the effect is truly incredible.

Your SPLASH when you dive in might seem small, but imagine the SPLASH caused by an orca as it deliberately creates waves and sends them rushing over the heads of hundreds of audience members a day, thousands a week, tens of thousands a month, and on and on.

When applied to public speaking, this is a reality that has the ability to change not only countless lives, but the whole world. If your dream matters, you've got to take a stand that will make a real difference, one that brings down rain on the heads of too many people to count—rain caused by your dedication to making the world better.

And if your dream doesn't matter enough for you to make SPLASHes in the right direction, listen to the sage advice of the muscled criminal from the Disney movie *Tangled:* "Your dream stinks!" And then go get a new dream!

This is what leadership means.

There are plenty of causes out there that matter, and you can't afford to latch on to one that doesn't deserve a SPLASH.

But let's be clear. Don't ever *actually* dive into a tank at Sea World. Seriously! But in the real world, there are puddles, tanks, and oceans for you to dive into, there are whales waiting to be given the sign that means, "SPLASH 'em till they don't know what hit 'em," and there are bleachers full of people tensed and ready for the onslaught of crashing water that only you can provide.

Go get 'em. It's time for a SPLASH! And you're the only one who can bring it!

# Other Books in the
# LIFE Leadership Essentials Series

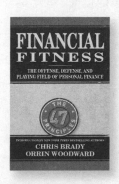

*Financial Fitness: The Offense, Defense, and Playing Field of Personal Finance* with Introduction by Chris Brady and Orrin Woodward – $21.95

If you ever feel that you're too far behind and can't envision a better financial picture, you are so WRONG! You need this book! The *Financial Fitness* book is for everyone at any level of wealth. Just like becoming physically or mentally fit, becoming financially fit requires two things: knowing what to do and taking the necessary action to do it. Learn how to prosper, conserve, and become fiscally fantastic. It's a money thing, and the power to prosper is all yours!

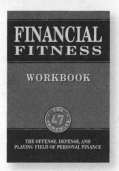

*Financial Fitness Workbook* – $7.95

Economic affairs don't have to be boring or stressful. Make managing money fun in a few simple steps. Use this workbook to get off to a great start and then continue down the right path to becoming fiscally fabulous! Discover exactly where all of your money actually goes as you make note of all your expenditures. Every page will put you one step closer to financial freedom, so purchase the *Financial Fitness Workbook* today and get budgeting!

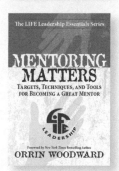

*Mentoring Matters: Targets, Techniques, and Tools for Becoming a Great Mentor* with Foreword by Orrin Woodward – $19.95

Get your sticky notes ready for all the info you're about to take in from this book. Do you know what it means to be a *great* mentor? It's a key part of successful leadership, but for most people, the necessary skills and techniques don't come naturally. Educate yourself on all of the key targets, techniques, and tools for becoming a magnificent mentor with this easy-to-apply manual. Your leadership success will be forever increased!

***Turn the Page: How to Read Like a Top Leader*** with **Introduction by Chris Brady – $15.95**
Leaders are readers. But there are many ways to read, and leaders read differently than most people do. They read to learn what they need to know, do, or feel, regardless of the author's intent or words. They see past the words and read with the specific intent of finding truth and applying it directly in their own lives. Learn how to read like a top leader so you'll be better able to emulate their success. Applying the skills taught in *Turn the Page* will impact your life, career, and leadership abilities in ways you can't even imagine. So turn the page and start reading!

# Subscriptions and
## Products from
# LIFE Leadership

**Rascal Radio Subscription – $49.95 per month**
**Rascal Radio** by LIFE Leadership is the world's first online personal development radio hot spot. Rascal Radio is centered on LIFE's 8 Fs: Faith, Family, Finances, Fitness, Following, Freedom, Friends, and Fun. Subscribers have unlimited access to **hundreds and hundreds** of audio recordings that they can stream endlessly from both the LIFE Leadership website and the **LIFE Leadership Smartphone App.** Listen to one of the preset stations or customize your own based on speaker or subject. Of course, you can easily skip tracks or "like" as many as you want. And if you are listening from the website, you can purchase any one of these incredible audios.

Let Rascal Radio provide you with **life-changing information to help you live the life you've always wanted!**

**The LIFE Series – $50.00 per month**
Here's where LIFE began—with the now famously followed 8 Fs: Family, Finances, Fitness, Faith, Following, Freedom, Friends, and Fun. This highly recommended series offers a strong foundation on which to build and advance in every area of your daily life. The timeless truths and effective strategies  included will reignite passion and inspire you to be your very best. Transform your life for the better and watch how it will create positive change in the lives of those around you. Subscribe today and have the time of your LIFE!

*Series includes 4 audios and 1 book monthly and is also available in Spanish and French.*

### The LLR (Launching a Leadership Revolution) Series – $50.00 per month

There is no such thing as a born leader. Based on the *New York Times* bestseller *Launching a Leadership Revolution* by Chris Brady and Orrin Woodward, this series focuses on teaching leadership skills at every level. The principles and specifics taught in the LLR Series will equip you with all the tools you need for business advancement, community influence, church impact, and even an advantage in your home life. Topics include: leadership, finances, public speaking, goal setting, mentoring, game planning, accountability and tracking of progress, levels of motivation and influence, and leaving a personal legacy. Will you be ready to take the lead when you're called? Subscribe now and learn how to achieve effective confidence skills while growing stronger in your leadership ability.

*Series includes 4 audios and 1 leadership book monthly.*

### The AGO (All Grace Outreach) Series – $25.00 per month

We are all here together to love one another and take care of each other. But sometimes in this hectic world, we lose our way and forget our true purpose. When you subscribe to the AGO Series, you'll gain the valuable support and guidance that every Christian searches for. Nurture your soul, strengthen your faith, and find answers to better understand God's plan for your life, marriage, and children.

*Series includes 1 audio and 1 book monthly.*

### The Edge Series – $10.00 per month

You'll cut in front of the rest of the crowd when you get the *Edge*. Designed for those on the younger side of life, this hard-core, no-frills series promotes self-confidence, drive, and motivation. Get advice, timely information, and true stories of success from interesting talks and fascinating people. Block out the noise around you and learn the principles of self-improvement at an early age. It's a gift that will keep on giving from parent to child. Subscribe today and get a competitive *Edge* on tomorrow.

*Series includes 1 audio monthly.*

### The Freedom Series – $10.00 per month

Freedom must be fought for if it is to be preserved. Every nation and generation needs people who are willing to take a stand for it. Are you one of those brave leaders who'll answer the call? Gain an even greater understanding of the significance and power of freedom, get better informed on issues that affect yours, and find out how you can prevent its decline.

This series covers freedom matters that are important to *you*. Make your freedom and liberty a priority and subscribe today.

*Series includes 1 audio monthly.*

### Financial Fitness Subscription – $10.00 per month for 12 months

If you found the *Financial Fitness Pack* life-changing and beneficial to your bank account, then you'll want even more timely information and guidance from the Financial Fitness Subscription. It's designed as a continuing economic education to help people develop financial discipline and overall knowledge of how their money works. Learn how to make financial principles your financial habits. It's a money thing, and it always pays to be cash savvy.

*Subscription includes 1 audio monthly.*

### LIFE Library Subscription – $40.00 per month

You'll never be shushed in this library. This online, round-the-clock resource is the best connection to LIFE's latest and greatest leadership content. You can watch or listen in either video or audio format, and easy access allows you to search by format, speaker, or subject. Go exploring through the entire content of the LIFE Library. Subscribe today, tune in, and turn it up.

**LIFE Live Subscription – $40.00 per month**
Are you missing out on LIFE? LIFE Live gives you an all-access pass to LIFE Seminars or Webinars all across North America. This cost-effective subscription lets you attend live gatherings in person or by viewing a LIFE Webinar from wherever you are. The LIFE/LLR Session kicks off these live events, which can range in size from a couple hundred to thousands of participants. Now you can continue to keep up with beneficial content and get the latest information you want. Subscribe today. We look forward to seeing you LIVE!

*Financial Fitness Pack* – **$99.99**
Once and for all, it's time to free yourself from the worry and heavy burden of debt. Decide today to take an honest look at your finances by learning and applying the simple principles of financial success. The *Financial Fitness Pack* provides you with all the tools needed to get on a path to becoming fiscally fantastic!

*Pack includes the* Financial Fitness *book, a companion workbook, and 8 audio recordings.*